A Spirit Deep Within

For Joom
From Joan.
Nice to Meet You

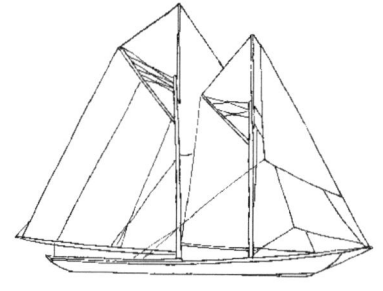

A Spirit Deep Within

Naval Architect W. J. Roué and the Bluenose Story

by Joan E. Roué

Vanwell Publishing Limited
St. Catharines, Ontario

Published 1995, New Edition 2002

Copyright © 2002

All rights reserved. No part of this book may be reproduced or used in any form or by any means, electronic or mechanical, including photocopying, recording, or in any information storage and retrieval system, without permission in writing from the publisher.

Vanwell Publishing acknowledges the financial support of the Government of Canada through the Book Publishing Industry Development Program for our publishing activities.

Cover Design by Renée Giguère

Vanwell Publishing Limited
1 Northrup Crescent
P.O. Box 2131
St. Catharines, Ontario L2R 7S2
sales@vanwell.com
tel: 905-937-3100
fax: 905-937-1760

Printed in Canada

National Library of Canada Cataloguing in Publication Data

Roué, Joan, 1961-
   A spirit deep within : naval architect W.J. Roué and the Bluenose story

Includes bibliographical references.
ISBN 1-55125-065-9

   1. Roué, William James, 1879-1970. 2. Bluenose (Ship) 3. Naval architects-Nova Scotia-Biography. I. Title.

VM140.R78R6 2002   623.8'122   C2002-901199-X

This book is respectfully and lovingly dedicated to Lawrence James Roué and Dorothy Mae Roué without whom this dream would never have become reality.

COVER PHOTOS
FRONT
W. J. Roué (1879-1970) circa 1930. *Roué family*

BACK
W. J. Roué commemorative postage stamp issued 1998. *Canada Post Corporation.*

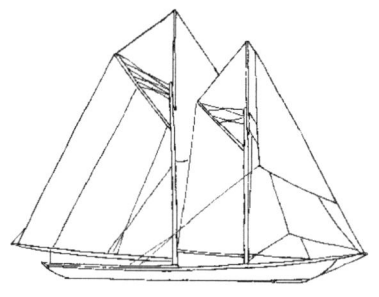

Contents

Preface *ix*

Part I

Introduction *3*
1 Soda Water to Salt Water *9*
2 Roué Plan #17 *15*
3 A Winning Design *19*
4 Surge of Success *23*
5 Launching a New Career *27*
6 Recognition All Around *31*
7 The War Years *35*
8 *Bluenose* Ghost *39*
9 The Spirit Lives On *43*
Epilogue *49*

Part II

How *Bluenose* Was Designed *63*
The Specifications of *Bluenose* *70*
The Roué 20 *77*

The *Bluenose* Class *78*
What Is A Bluenose? *80*
Appendix
   Highlights: W. J. Roué *81*
   W. J. Roué Designs *84*
   Highlights: *Bluenose* *95*
   Bluenose Racing Log *97*
   Highlights: *Bluenose II* *100*

References *102*
Acknowledgements *104*
New Since 1995 *105*
BLUENOSE II Highlights *109*
William J. Roué Highlights *110*

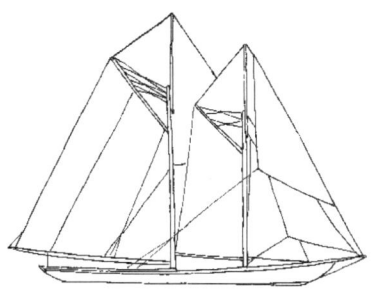

Preface

It is with great pleasure that I present this story. For many years I have yearned to see something of its kind in print: a precise and brief account of this integral chapter of our Maritime history. But what could I add to the saga of *Bluenose* that had not been told before?

I have always felt especially close to *Bluenose* because her designer, William James Roué, was my great-grandfather. He lived in Dartmouth, Nova Scotia, just a couple of miles from our home. I can remember quite vividly my father taking me to visit his grandfather, and I would sit on the knee of this calm, peaceful old man. Being only a young child, I did not realize how precious these moments were; I had no concept of life and death. When I was nine years old, my great-grandfather passed away.

After I began school, I gained some sense that my great-grandfather was different—he was respected for some distinctive accomplishment. Teachers would hear my surname and usually realize I was a descendant of W. J. Roué. I developed great pride in this fact.

Throughout my life I would never know when the tie

would be recognized. It could happen at any occasion, from a business meeting to social gatherings. Upon introducing myself, I would often hear: "Roué . . . any relation to . . . ?" As often I would get mispronunciations such as Roo, Roe, Rooay, and so on. The correct pronunciation is Ru-ee.

After the death of my great-grandfather, I was very fortunate to hear stories from my grandfather James Frederick Roué, and my father, Lawrence (Laurie) James Roué. Both were very close to, and travelled with, W. J. Roué throughout much of his career.

Known as Bill to his friends, W. J. Roué became one of the best known naval architects in the Western Hemisphere. The original *Bluenose* is the most famous vessel built to his design, but the Roué yachts and schooners are well respected, and still sailing throughout North America today.

Then again W. J. Roué was a very humble man. He did not feel he had accomplished anything extraordinary. From the family stories, I developed a great respect for the man and his craft, and concluded that he, like *Bluenose*, gained his strength from a spirit deep within.

But I have often felt that my great-grandfather deserved greater recognition in this day and age—not only for designing *Bluenose* and his other well loved classes of boats— but also for the sheer breadth of a remarkable career, and his pioneering role as a Canadian naval architect.

Thus, when the Nova Scotia government announced its intention to permanently dock *Bluenose II* in March of 1994, my interest in my great-grandfather's story revived. I became preoccupied with it; I travelled, read, and researched, looking for any tidbits available.

Why? Because I wanted to tell the stories of *Bluenose* and *Bluenose II* from a new perspective: through the life and career of their designer, William James Roué.

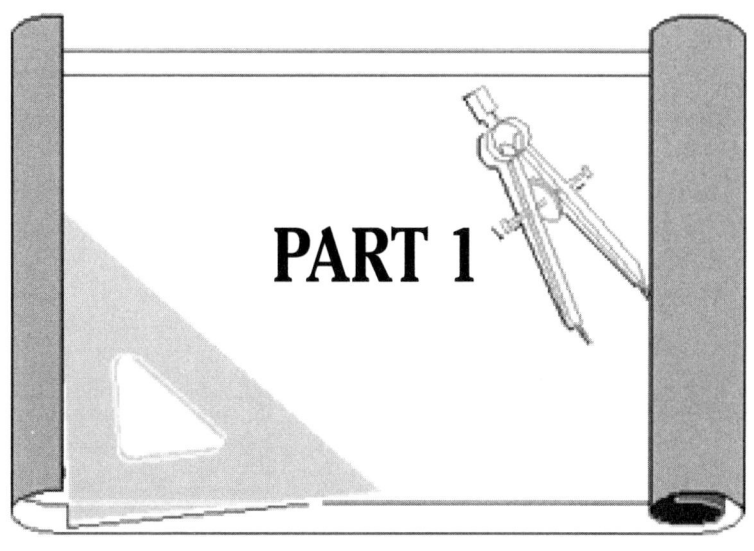

PART 1

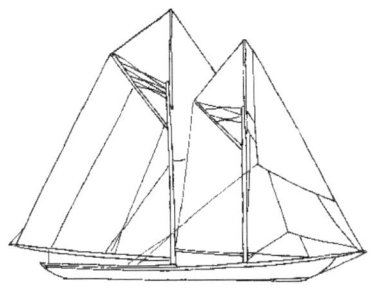

Introduction

It was October 1938. Canadians from coast to coast were beaming with pride: their schooner *Bluenose* had once again defeated the American entry, *Gertrude L. Thebaud*, for the International Fishermen's Trophy. The two vessels had been tied going into the fifth and deciding race of the International Fishermen's races, yet the aging *Bluenose* had responded to the challenge, and had kept the trophy in Canada.

The series of 1938 was, in a sense, a tie breaker. They had met twice before: once in 1930, for the Sir Thomas Lipton Series, and then in 1931, for the International Fishermen's series. *Gertrude L. Thebaud* had beaten *Bluenose* in 1930, but *Bluenose* had been victorious in 1931. The 1938 victory assured *Bluenose* that she would be known forever as Queen of the North Atlantic. Little did everyone realize, however, that *Bluenose* would never race again; that the competition and victory of 1938 would be her last.

But what had made her the champion she was? Who was this *Bluenose* who had united Canadians from the Atlantic to the Pacific, and had encouraged a spirited rivalry between Canada and the United States? How did this magnificent vessel come to be?

Turning to the sea
The town of Lunenburg, Nova Scotia, became one of the greatest fishing ports and shipbuilding centres of the world. The road to such a distinction, however, was a long and varied one.

In the 1750s, the British Crown wanted more Protestant colonists in Nova Scotia to help offset the French and Catholic influence. King George II sought candidates for immigration from French states, Switzerland, and his native Germany, encouraging them with the same incentives of land and supplies as he offered to his English subjects.

Many accepted, and within three years, nearly 3,000 "foreign Protestants" had arrived in Halifax. Mostly farmers, and unlike other residents in their language and customs, the new, mostly German-speaking immigrants, chose to form settlements together. In 1753, about half moved to what would become the Lunenburg area, called Merligash at the time, on Nova Scotia's South Shore, west of Halifax, where they endured Indian raids, privateers, and fierce winter storms.

It was not long before the transplanted German-speaking farmers realized there was a much greater harvest to be reaped from the surrounding salt waters than from the soils of this new land. Lunenburg Harbour was sheltered, opening into the sprawling waters of the Atlantic Ocean. So by the 1850s, men of Lunenburg had established their reputations as boat builders and fishermen, and were regularly sailing to the Grand Banks off the Newfoundland coast, and beyond, to the icy waters between Greenland and Iceland.

They sailed in a vessel called the schooner, also known as a salt banker, because in it, they caught and salted fish on the Banks. From spring to autumn each year, the schooners would sail out to the Grand Banks, their decks stacked with the characteristic silhouette of wooden dories. The dories would be lowered over the sides of the schooners at dawn, manned by two hardy mariners. Trawl lines about a mile and a half long were set out and checked for fish four times each day before the men returned to the schooner at dusk.

These ships had to be seaworthy on the rough waters of the North Atlantic, yet light-footed as they raced to their home ports once the holds were full. The first schooner in usually got the best prices.

Racing schooners
During the 1850s, a great rivalry developed between British and American yachts. The Royal Yacht Squadron of England sponsored a trophy for the One Hundred Guineas Cup, a 60–mile race around the Isle of Wight. The Americans won the trophy in 1851 with their entry, *America*, and the name of the race became the America's Cup. Thirteen times British adversaries tried and failed to regain the cup. It is said that over $75 million was spent by British yachtsmen in those early years in quest of the America's Cup.

While this gentlemen's sporting competition was taking place between the British and Americans, the Grand Banks fishing schooners were racing to their home ports of Lunenburg, Nova Scotia, and Gloucester, Massachusetts. Although these races were not official, they were definitely taken seriously. The fishermen watched the America's Cup races with contempt. In their opinion, fortunes were being wasted on these useless yachts.

The postponement of the 1920 America's Cup race, due to strong winds, prompted Senator William H. Dennis, owner of the *Halifax Herald* and *Evening Mail* newspapers in Halifax, Nova Scotia, to sponsor a new series between working vessels of the Canadian and U.S. fishing fleets. The new competition boasted a huge cup, the International Fishing Vessel Championship Trophy (or the International Fishermen's Trophy as it came to be called), for the winning vessel.

Competitors had to be authentic Canadian and American working fishing boats. There were general specifications, and all entries had to have spent at least one fishing season on the Banks. Each series would be captured by the vessel winning the best two out of three races. The competition site would alternate between Halifax and Gloucester.

Grand Banks fishermen eagerly anticipated the new series, as did citizens from both countries. Americans held their elimination races off Gloucester, while the Canadians sailed off Halifax to determine their entry.

On October 20, and November 1, 1920, the respective winners, *Delawana* representing Canada, and the American entry, *Esperanto*, met off Halifax in the first ever races for the International Fishermen's Trophy. Much to the chagrin of Canadians, *Esperanto* won. The people of Canada vowed to bring the trophy back home.

Taking action to ensure the fulfillment of this pledge was a group of Nova Scotia businessmen, headed by a well-known captain, Angus Walters, from Lunenburg. A planning committee formed The Bluenose Schooner Company. They needed a vessel that would be both a racer and an able worker, earning her keep as both. Their schooner would need the cargo carrying capacity of a salt-banker, and the speed of a fresh fisherman.

But who would design her? The Bluenose Schooner Company knew that the best American and British designers were using mathematical calculations to produce blueprints from which their yachts were built. Most shipbuilders in Canada worked out their designs from wooden half models, modifying them to suit the ship's captain. To have an American naval architect design the Canadian challenger was unthinkable, but who in Canada could apply the new mathematical methods to produce the plans for a winning design?

One of the members of the group knew of a young Dartmouth man who had gained a reputation locally, both for his skilled handling of yachts, and for the yachts he had designed for members of the Royal Nova Scotia Yacht Squadron in Halifax. His name was William James Roué, or Bill, as he was called by most.

Roué family business ad, 1895. *1895 Halifax City Directory*

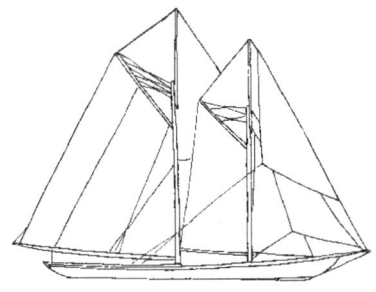

1. Soda Water to Salt Water

Although a longtime resident of Dartmouth, Nova Scotia, William James Roué was actually born across the harbour in the seaport of Halifax, Nova Scotia, on April 27, 1879. He was the second son of James and Grace (Penaligan) Roué.

Bill's father was a descendant of a Huguenot family, de la Roué, who had escaped from France and settled in Barnstaple, England in 1603. This branch of the Roué family, which contained a tangle of Jameses and Johns, migrated to Nova Scotia early in the 19th century.

The first generation of Roués in Nova Scotia settled in Dartmouth. James Roué, a barber, was father to second generation James Roué, a manufacturer of soda water who moved across the harbour. He operated his business, Roué's Carbonated Waters, Ltd., at 121 Lower Water Street, Woods Wharf, on the Halifax waterfront. James, his wife, Grace, and their three children, William, John, and Harold, lived nearby on Kent Street, in Halifax.

Roué's Carbonated Waters, Ltd. was an old established

and well-known business of Halifax. It had been founded in 1851 as Baker & Co. James Roué's brother, John, acquired the business in 1879, and continued to use the Baker name for a time. Eventually he gave the firm his family name.

When John Roué died in 1883, James Roué bought his brother's company. The 1895 Halifax City Directory lists the company description as "James Roué, Soda Water Manufacturer." By 1914, the description had become "James Roué, Carbonated Beverages and Soda Water Manufacturers."

James Roué was one of the early pioneers of soft drinks in North America, and one of the original producers of Canadian ginger ale. He was a talented man, a bit of an inventor himself, and a courtly gentleman of the old school. Although he was an engineer, James Roué was down to earth. He would not hesitate to take off his coat and roll up his sleeves to help his employees in a time of need. He was always on the lookout for new ideas to enhance the quality and desirability of his products.

The Wood's Wharf premises comprised four floors, each 84x75 feet. They were equipped with all the most up-to-date steam and electrically operated machinery. The plant had an annual capacity of 50,000 dozen bottles. In addition to a large local city business, Roué's Carbonated Waters, Ltd. continued to expand steadily throughout the province as country customers were acquired

Roué's Carbonated Waters, Ltd. manufactured a general line of carbonated beverages, specializing in ginger ale. Their ginger ale had been pronounced by connoisseurs to be equal to the best imported from Britain. Roué soda waters won first prize in the 1891 and 1894 Provincial Exhibitions, as well as first prize for excellence and purity at the Dominion and Provincial Exhibitions of 1881. Their recipes were sold to other manufacturers in both the United States and Great

Britain. Today, the distinctive Roué bottles are collectors' items, and worth anywhere between $15 and $500.

James's second son, William James, demonstrated very early that he preferred salt water to soda water. When he was only four years old, Bill started making toy boats out of any wood thin enough for him to cut. At five, he brought a model to James and asked him to put lead outside ballast on it. Few naval architects were using outside ballast then, so young W. J. Roué was certainly one of the early experimenters with this concept.

By the time he was 13, Bill Roué was making five-foot model sailing yachts. They sailed so fast that two men rowing a light skiff could not catch them. He haunted the Royal Nova Scotia Yacht Squadron, and was an expert yacht skipper even before he became a member.

Bill Roué was formally educated at the County Academy in Halifax, Nova Scotia. A student who shared a desk with Roué said that Bill would have been a good student, particularly in mathematics, had he paid more attention to the teachers instead of spending his time drawing yachts.

During these early years, Bill Roué learned to save every scrap of information he could find on naval architecture. He studied diligently in the Yacht Squadron's unheated library when the club was closed to the public. He created many sketches of vessels and, eager for advice, showed them to local yachtsmen.

Halifax City Solicitor, Frank H. Bell, also a Yacht Squadron member, took notice of the keen, young Mr. Roué, and gave him an old edition of Dixon-Kemp (*Yachting Architecture*), the naval architect's bible. Bill studied the pages thoroughly, literally wearing the volumes to a frazzle. But he knew their contents almost by heart and could recognize instantly any yacht described therein.

As a result of his studies, Bill Roué made his first mathematically calculated design, Plan #1, a motor boat. It is not known if this boat was ever built.

In 1895, at the age of 16, Bill Roué left school, and accepted a position as a junior clerk for the wholesale grocery firm of Bauld and Gibson in Halifax. At the same time, he took night classes in mechanical drafting at the Victoria School of Art and Design, now the Nova Scotia College of Art and Design (NSCAD).

Earning $100 annually as a junior clerk, 18-year-old Bill Roué used $10 dollars to join the Royal Nova Scotia Yacht Squadron. With another $16 he replaced his worn Dixon-Kemp.

During this period, Bill entered several yacht designs in competitions sponsored by *Rudder* magazine. He won honourable mention. Looking back through these old publications years later, even Bill Roué, the most modest man his friends ever knew, had to admit that his boat designs were as good as any.

Bill worked at Bauld and Gibson until he joined the family firm, Roué's Carbonated Waters, Ltd., as a full time junior clerk in 1903. He was 24. He worked diligently with his father, and his brother, John, to learn about the family business. His brother, Harold, reported to be able to add instantly an entire page of figures in his head, became an accountant. In subsequent years, Bill Roué learned to prepare the extracts, and developed the formula for a very dry ginger ale, named Bluenose.

In 1907, Frank H. Bell, vice commodore of the Royal Nova Scotia Yacht Squadron, decided he wanted a larger boat. He made a sketch of what he had in mind, and approached Bill Roué. If Bill would design the boat, Frank said he would consider having it built. Roué, just 28, agreed, and set to work to draw up the plans for his first sailing yacht.

That fall, Frank Bell journeyed to Boston on business. He carried the Roué plans with him to show to a close friend, B. B. Crowninshield, one of America's foremost naval architects. The conversation was said to have gone like this: "Frank, who drew these plans?" "Oh, a young amateur from home who sails with me." "Well," Ben Crowninshield replied, "he won't be an amateur for long. Go ahead and build, you will never regret it."

And so *Babette* was born. She was built in a boat shed near the Canadian National rail station on Hollis Street in Halifax. *Babette* was launched in the spring of 1909, and was still sailing out of a port on Long Island, New York, in 1970.

With the design of *Babette* in 1907, the career of W. J. Roué, naval architect, unofficially began. Over the next 11 years Bill would complete 14 more designs, mostly yachts, while still working full time at the family firm. Prior to this period, it is generally believed that most Canadian yacht designs were taken off wooden half models. Only those Canadian vessels built to designs from the U.S. or Great Britain used blueprints. At 28, W. J. Roué had become a Canadian pioneer in naval architecture.

In 1908, Bill Roué married the former Winnifred Conrod of Halifax. She had received recognition as a teacher at the School for the Deaf, in Halifax. Winnifred had been compared to Annie Sullivan, Helen Keller's teacher, because she developed a remarkable rapport with her students who progressed quickly under her exceptional tutelage.

Bill and Winnifred had four children: James Frederick (Jim), twins Harry, and William F. (who died at birth), and Frances Grace. The Roués lived the greatest part of their married life on James Street in Dartmouth, overlooking Halifax Harbour. Their house still stands at number 23 today.

In the fall of 1920, when he was 41, and his children were still young, W. J. Roué accepted a challenge that would bring him world-wide acclaim, and change the course of his life forever.

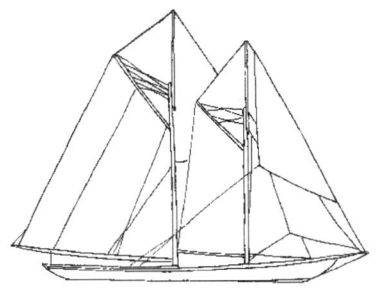

2. Roué Plan #17

Bill Roué was working full time at the family soda factory when the Bluenose Schooner Company's planning committee approached him to design their vessel for the International Fishermen's race. Bill had never designed a fishing schooner, but boat designing was his passion, something he had taught himself, and worked on after hours. How could he refuse such a challenge?

Bill Roué accepted the task, confident of his abilities. The only technical guideline he received was that the vessel had to be 120 feet on the waterline. Working laboriously at night throughout the fall of 1920, Bill produced the vessel he thought would beat the existing contenders. He submitted his design three weeks early.

The committee rejected his plans because the vessel was too long, even though it met their original specifications. They asked Roué to cut the length down to 112 feet on the waterline. Cut it down! This was an unreasonable request to Bill Roué. Each of his boats was a separate creation; each design an individual inspiration.

Immediately Bill began all over again, and still managed to complete the new design within the three-week deadline. The committee accepted his design this time, and it was to become *Bluenose*, Roué Plan #17.

The Bluenose Schooner Company sold shares all over Canada to raise the estimated $35,000 needed to build *Bluenose*. Captain Angus Walters, of Lunenburg, was invited to command her, and Zwicker & Company, also of Lunenburg, was named as agents.

A shipyard in Lunenburg, Smith and Rhuland Shipyards., founded in 1900, was awarded the contract to build *Bluenose*. It was reported that the owners of Smith and Rhuland Shipyards, a firm which had already built more than 100 fishing schooners in its yards, were aghast at the idea of building a schooner using blueprints.

The keel was laid late in 1920. To mark the beginning of construction, the Duke of Devonshire, Governor General of Canada, drove a golden spike into the keel. Apparently he had arrived early that day, and had sampled some of the local brew. According to hearsay, by the time he appeared for the ceremony, the Duke was barely able to focus on the golden spike, let alone drive it home.

So, the building of *Bluenose* began. The best shipwrights were assembled to work on her. The materials used in construction were entirely Nova Scotian, except the Douglas fir from British Columbia used for the spars. The construction methods used on *Bluenose* were similar to all other schooners built in the yard, but the design was radically different.

Bill Roué visited the shipyard often to see that his plans were being followed as the vessel was being constructed. This was typical of Roué as it was his policy to reserve the right of "first and last refusal" for each and every design: he would not agree to work on a project if he could not personally ensure that each aspect of the venture was completed to his satisfaction.

Ernest (Ern) Bell of Halifax, a lifelong friend of W. J. Roué, accompanied him to Smith and Rhuland Shipyards during the construction of *Bluenose*. On one such visit after *Bluenose* was in frame, a worker told Ernest Bell: "We are building her as close to your friend's lines as we know how. If she's a success he gets the praise; if she's a failure he gets the blame."

Over the years, some have suggested that there may have been changes made to the lines of *Bluenose* which were not true to W. J. Roué's plans. Ern Bell insisted that the worker's comments on that day, and his own observations at the shipyard on the same day, pretty much settled the matter: as *Bluenose* was in frame by then, no alteration would have been possible.

On another of his many visits to Lunenburg during the construction period, Bill Roué said, "Mr. Rhuland, I don't like the way you're doing the rudder. It's too thick at the after edge." George Rhuland replied that they always did a fishing schooner's rudder that way. To which Bill responded with a whisper: "Did you ever see a trout with a square tail?" Mr. Rhuland took the point with good humour, then directed his son, John, to rework the rudder according to the designer's instructions. After a few days' work, John's efforts satisfied Bill Roué.

The only alteration made to Roué's plans was at the request of Captain Angus Walters, who wanted to give the crew more room. Being practical, Bill Roué thought this was a good idea for a couple of reasons: first, it would give the crew more comfort; secondly, "There was a big difference between a foot of water on your deck and none at all."

With the consent of the designer, the forecastle (fo'c's'le) was raised a foot. In doing this, the most forward part of the upper deck was made a full 12 inches higher; the topside of the ship also became another 12 inches above the waterline. It was this adjustment that gave *Bluenose* her distinguished nose.

Did this change affect her speed? Because of the alteration was she faster, slower? Her designer thought it may have slowed her slightly. Perhaps if she had been built to the original plan, *Bluenose* would have been even faster yet.

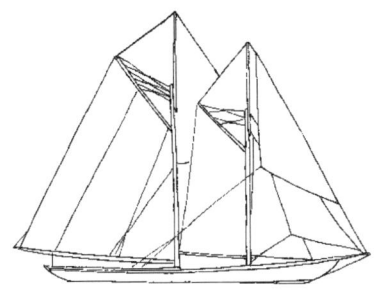

3. A Winning Design

Bluenose was launched on March 26, 1921. She was a fisherman, but a fisherman deluxe. She carried aboard many luxuries previously unknown to other vessels of the fishing fleet.

The cabin of Captain Angus Walters was furnished with a brass bed and fitted with electric lights and bells. A complete electrical system ran throughout the entire vessel.

The main cabin could accommodate eight men, with the captain's quarters located in a smaller recess off this compartment. In the forecastle, she had quarters for 16 men, two more than provided in most vessels of her type. In general, her accommodations were spacious, second to none in the fleet.

She was 270 tons deadweight and could carry 2,600 quintals of fish. A gasoline auxiliary engine for hoisting the sails, her eight dories, and other fishing equipment made Bluenose a valuable addition to the fleet.

Ballasted, rigged, outfitted, and provisioned, Bluenose sailed for the Grand Banks on April 15, 1921. Her maiden voyage was a fishing trip, as she needed to qualify as a genuine fisherman before she could compete for the International Fishermen's Trophy.

An uneventful trip it was not. One night, as *Bluenose* sat anchored on the Banks, a full rigged ship bore down on her. Captain Walters struck the bell and blasted the fog horn repeatedly, but the other ship did not change course. He gave the order to abandon ship and *Bluenose* crewmen went over the sides in dories. They were sure *Bluenose* would be cut in two. The other vessel missed *Bluenose* by inches in what they called a miracle. The identity of the other ship was never established.

Bluenose returned to Lunenburg as highliner of the fleet that summer of 1921, a title earned by the vessel having the biggest catch of fish. It would also be the largest catch recorded in Lunenburg during the 1920s.

Bluenose was then refitted and readied to compete in her first official racing competition. As last minute preparations were made for the eliminations, Captain Walters and W. J. Roué were personally overseeing the work. Dressed in oilskins, Roué helped relocate the ballast himself.

The American victor from the previous year, *Esperanto*, had unfortunately been lost at sea. *Mayflower* was chosen by the Americans to defend the International Fishermen's Trophy. However, she was disqualified on the grounds that she was not a real fisherman, but a racing schooner in disguise. In the end, *Elsie* was the American ship named to compete in the quest for the 1921 International Fishermen's Trophy.

The trial races had been held in Canada also. *Bluenose* clearly demonstrated her superiority over her Canadian competitors. She was especially strong sailing to windward.

Excitement was high in Halifax in anticipation of the schooner races. The Dartmouth Ferry Commission even scheduled excursions to take enthusiasts to watch the contest.

Thousands of people lined the shores and boarded the ferries on October 22, 1921, to watch as *Bluenose* defeated *Elsie* by more than 13 minutes in the first race. Captain Angus Walters commented, "She did exactly what I expected her to do, and given a decent wind next Saturday, she'll repeat the performance." W. J. Roué was equally pleased, saying, "I am more proud of her ability as a fisherman than as a speedster. She has proven herself to be everything that was expected." He was confident that Marty Welch, captain of *Elsie*, was going to have the race of his life in the second event. Given equal conditions, Roué could see no reason why *Bluenose* should not do even better than she did in the first match.

From the outset, Captain Angus Walters laid the foundation of an honourable career for *Bluenose*. During the first race of this initial series, *Elsie* lost her fore topmast on the leg home. Captain Walters saw the situation at once, and refused to take advantage of it: he ordered his crew to take down the sails on *Bluenose's* fore topmast. Although he wanted *Bluenose* to win the race, Captain Walters wanted her to deserve it.

Between the races *Bluenose* crew did not rest on their laurels. Early the next morning they gave the sails their final overhauling. After a trial spin following her victory in the first race, Captain Walters and W. J. Roué decided that her ballast would not be touched. They were well satisfied with her trim, and would leave well enough alone. Under these racing conditions, those who sailed her were finally able to appreciate the true details of the handling of *Bluenose*.

As predicted, the second race on October 24 ended with the same result, but this time *Bluenose* had a margin of victory of more than three miles. Canada had won back the

International Fishermen's Trophy and *Bluenose* fever ripped the country!

The stage was now set for a friendly, but fierce rivalry between the United States of America and Canada. Citizens from across both countries became involved in the challenge.

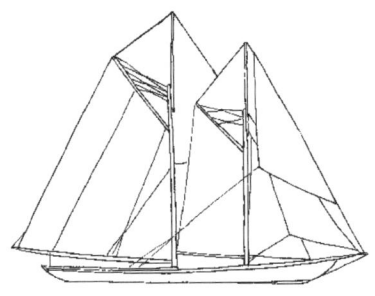

4. Surge of Success

Bluenose easily won the preliminary races in Halifax the following year, and sailed for Gloucester, the site of the 1922 International Fishermen's competition. She was to defend her title against the new American vessel, *Henry Ford*, especially designed to beat *Bluenose*. Betting men and confident sailors all along the eastern seaboard of the U.S. were sure *Henry Ford* would bring the trophy back to them.

American hopes were high as *Henry Ford* won the first race in a light wind, on October 23, 1922. But the second race had stronger gusts, and *Bluenose* won. The third race had winds of over 25 knots (more than it took to postpone the 1920 America's Cup) and *Bluenose* was in her glory. Once again she triumphed and returned home to Nova Scotia with the trophy.

Now that *Bluenose* was a success, everyone tried to claim the credit. Ernest Bell once said, "That used to make me so mad that I wanted to blow off but Bill just grinned and said 'Let them rave'." He once asked W. J. Roué the secret of *Bluenose*. Roué simply answered "I gave her the power to carry sail."

Roué permitted one of the yachting magazines to publish the lines of *Bluenose*. In the article, a professor George Owen stated: "There has been a great deal of claptrap talked about this beautiful vessel. There is no mystery of her performance. She is a superlatively good adaptation of the well known laws governing naval architecture. Look at her beautiful entrance and her long clean run."

In 1921, W. J. Roué had received a scroll from the citizens of Dartmouth, Nova Scotia, which expressed their thanks to the designer of *Bluenose* for bringing fame and honour to Dartmouth. It was among the first in a long line of honours Bill Roué would receive. The scroll read as follows:

> The Citizens of Dartmouth being proud of the fact that a fellow citizen had the inspiration and courage necessary to undertake the creation of the marvelous 'Bluenose', winner of the International schooner race at Halifax October 24, 1921, take great pleasure in rendering congratulations and wish you to know their appreciation of the honor conferred on the town. Words fail to express the pleasure of beholding the result of your handiwork during the elimination races and the grand historical sailing duel with the noble 'Elsie', pride of the American fleet. As a token of esteem and admiration they ask your kind acceptance of a gift which may be found helpful for timing the speed of future contenders for the International Championship'.
> Dartmouth, N.S.
> Dec. 30, 1921
> On behalf of the Citizens

The gift was a gold pocket watch. Engraved on the outside cover was a broadside view of *Bluenose*, in full sail. On the inside was an inscription from the Town of Dartmouth. Bill Roué treasured this gift forever.

It was in 1922 that one of W. J. Roué's new designs, #20, the Star Class yacht, attracted not only local, but national attention. The stem of the yacht caught the eye of all boat fans: it was a miniature adaptation of the famous racing schooner, *Bluenose*. This class later became known as the Roué 20.

The first two Star Class yachts took up their moorings in the North West Arm of Halifax Harbour, and for weeks kept the surrounding waters filled with canoes, rowboats, and dinghies loaded with admiring yacht lovers.

By 1923, the Americans had built another fishing vessel with the International Fishermen's Trophy in mind. *Columbia* was designed by well–known naval architect, W. Starling Burgess, who later designed many winning vessels in other racing competitions. *Columbia* won her elimination races, easily defeating *Henry Ford* and other entries.

Captain Ben Pine was *Columbia's* skipper. He was renowned as one of the most skillful captains ever to sail out of Gloucester. *Columbia* was a shade smaller than *Bluenose*, equally as graceful, and had just as great a fish carrying capacity. Ben Pine and Captain Walters had been friends for many years.

Halifax was the site of the International Fishermen's races of 1923. *Bluenose* won the first race on October 29. A few days later, in the second race, *Bluenose* crossed the finish line first. However, the captain of *Columbia* registered a complaint with the series committee.

Captain Pine said that *Bluenose*, under the command of his friend Captain Walters, had passed *Columbia* inside a navigation buoy. *Bluenose* was therefore disqualified, and the trophy should be given to *Columbia*. Captain Walters, on the other hand, contended that he had not passed inside the buoy, and as *Bluenose* had won two races, the trophy belonged to her.

So much arguing ensued that the committee called off the series that year, split the prize money between the two vessels, and kept possession of the trophy. It would remain with them until 1931, as there would be no official International Fishermen's races for the next eight years.

Captain Angus Walters often said that *Bluenose* actually had her greatest performance in the spring of 1926. As she lay anchored off the coast of Sable Island (east south east of Halifax), long known for its terrible storms and lucrative catches, a sudden gale enveloped her. For eight hours the storm pounded the ship and its crew. Blinding snow and fierce seas battered them, breaking *Bluenose* free from her cable. Captain Walters lashed himself to the wheel while the crew fought for their lives. Finally the storm moved on. *Bluenose* had defeated Mother Nature.

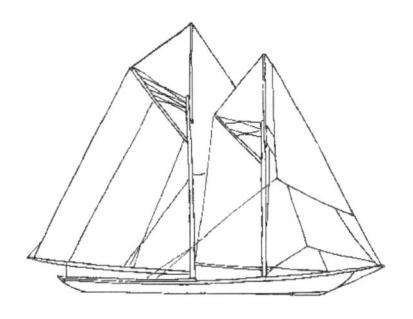

5. Launching a New Career

In the meantime, the Americans weren't the only ones attempting to create a schooner that could beat *Bluenose*. A group of shippers from Shelburne, Nova Scotia, commissioned W. J. Roué to design them a fishing schooner to compete in the Canadian eliminations for the International Fishermen's races.

As *Bluenose* was at her worst in light going, Roué thought the new vessel should be at her best in those conditions. The new design was built at Shelburne Shipbuilders Limited, under the direction of James Harding, recognized as one of the best in the trade at that time. Her name was *Haligonian*.

The two ships met in the elimination races held in October, 1926. The grand old lady, *Bluenose*, defeated her new challenger readily. However, it was said that *Haligonian's* sails did not fit well at the time.

Later, after running aground in the Canso Strait, *Haligonian* was sent to Lunenburg to be reballasted, and refitted with a new keel and proper sails.

Following this work, *Haligonian* raced *Bluenose* once again in a Lunenburg fishermen's race, and this time she beat *Bluenose* by a good nine minutes. However, the two ships never met again.

James Roué, Bill's father, had passed away in 1924. Bill, 45, became president of Roué's Carbonated Waters, Ltd., and ran the company with his brother, John, until 1929, when they sold the firm to the Bluenose Beverage Company.

That same year, largely as a result of the success of *Bluenose*, Bill decided at last to follow his heart; he switched to naval architecture as his true profession. W. J. Roué hung out his architect's shingle at an office on Barrington Street, in downtown Halifax, although he remained as a consultant to Bluenose Beverage until 1934.

One of Bill's first professional commissions was the design for a three–masted schooner, to be used as a training ship by the Canadian Navy. The vessel was named *H.M.C.S. Venture*.

During the late '20s, Bill Roué began designing boats built by James Harding, and Shelburne Shipbuilders Limited. The vessels were primarily yachts for customers in the United States. The Payne brokerage firm in New York had five of these built. One was also designed and built for Molson Breweries of Montréal.

A cruising schooner, *Malay*, also a Roué design, won the Bermuda race twice, once in her own class in 1928, and again in 1930, when she defeated the whole fleet. *Malay* was the only Canadian vessel to do so.

In 1930, Bill Roué submitted a design for an eight metre racing yacht as a contender for the Canada Cup. His design was chosen over applicants from across Canada. This was one of the few racing designs he created. It had to conform to page after page of international rules which made other designs appear a simple task. This yacht, *Norseman*, was later built at the Royal Canadian Yacht Club in Toronto, and became the champion of the Great Lakes.

Little Haligonian, a 46-foot schooner from the Roué drawing board, won the St. Petersburg to Havana classic eight times before she was burned at sea about 1940.

Meanwhile, south of the border, Americans were once again preparing to face Roué's first winner, *Bluenose*. In New England, the result of the 1923 International Fishermen's races still smarted. A group of sportsmen commissioned Frank Payne, a Boston naval architect, to design yet another challenger for *Bluenose*.

Similar to the guidelines Bill Roué had originally received in 1920, Payne was contracted to design a schooner that could not only fish and make money, but, most importantly, could defeat *Bluenose!* Arthur Story, of Essex, Massachusetts, built this new vessel. She was *Gertrude L. Thebaud*, or *Thebaud* as she was called.

Launched in 1930, *Gertrude L. Thebaud* was about six feet shorter in length than *Bluenose*, and only carried about 7,700 feet of sail, compared to *Bluenose's* 10,000. Of fine lines, *Gertrude L. Thebaud* showed great speed. She was a worthy rival, and was captained by *Columbia's* master, Captain Ben Pine, who was the manager of the coalition which owned the vessel.

Bluenose and *Thebaud* met off Gloucester in 1930. Sir Thomas Lipton sponsored the trophy and prize money. The competition was known as the Lipton Cup. Both parties agreed that the International Fishermen's Trophy was not at stake. *Thebaud* won both races. Captain Walters congratulated Captain Pine, admitting that *Bluenose* had been fairly beaten.

The next year, in 1931, the two schooners decided to meet for the International Fishermen's Trophy. The races were held off Halifax. *Bluenose* easily won the first two of the series, rendering her the victor. This was a huge disappointment to the enthusiastic Americans who were sure their *Gertrude L. Thebaud* would finally bring the International Fishermen's Trophy back to Gloucester.

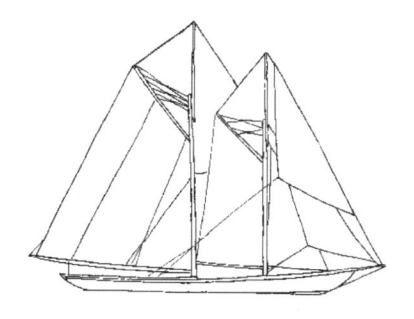

6. Recognition All Around

It was in 1931 that William J. Roué was included in *Prominent Men of Canada,* a publication featuring biographies of current outstanding Canadian citizens.

Bill concluded his consulting work with the Bluenose Beverage Company in 1934 to become a full-time naval architect, and soon received an offer from a prestigious naval architecture firm in the United States. As a result, Mr. and Mrs. W. J. Roué, their family grown, left Dartmouth to live in City Island, New York, for a brief period in the mid-'30s. There, Bill was a partner in the firm of Ford, Payne, and W. J. Roué.

In October, 1936, Bill and Winnifred returned to Dartmouth. During their absence, the family home had been occupied and cared for by family members. Apparently, the fast paced lifestyle of New York City had not agreed with the Roués, and they were thankful to be back home where they "had time to think."

Bluenose was also receiving considerable recognition. Now a world renowned celebrity, she was immortalized on January 6, 1929, when the Canadian government issued a 50¢

commemorative stamp in her honour. Pale blue in colour, the stamp shows *Bluenose* broadside, with sails full and one rail under water. Another vessel in head–on view, is supposed to be *Columbia*, in the 1923 International Fishermen's races. In fact, this schooner is also *Bluenose*. Based on a composite of images by Nova Scotian photographer W. R. MacAskill, this stamp was said to be one of the most beautiful, and intricately designed stamps ever produced in Canada.

Bluenose was invited to represent Canada at the Chicago World's Fair of 1933, formally called the Century of Progress Exposition. In order to accommodate the journey up the St. Lawrence River and through the Great Lakes, her keel had to be altered. On the journey home, *Bluenose* stopped in Toronto. She stayed the winter, allowing thousands to visit her over the period.

Her keel restored, *Bluenose* sailed to England in 1935, to take part in the Silver Jubilee celebrations of King George V and Queen Mary, marking 25 years of their reign. *Bluenose* was placed in line at the Spithead Review of the Royal Navy. King George, grandfather to Her Majesty Queen Elizabeth II, came aboard to visit Captain Walters, presenting him with a set of sails.

Soon after leaving England, *Bluenose* was nearly lost at sea in a heavy gale. She sprang a leak near the stern, and limped back to Plymouth. After repairs, she journeyed safely home to Lunenburg.

The Age of Sail was quickly coming to an end with the onset of more efficient diesel engines to power the fishing vessels. In 1936, in the interest of remaining commercially competitive, the owners of *Bluenose* installed a diesel engine and removed her sails. She returned to the Banks and took her place beside the other fishing vessels.

Just when she had had her sails clipped, *Bluenose* appeared in full sail on the back of the Canadian dime. This newest honour from the government and people of Canada occurred on January 1, 1937, when the coin, again based on a photograph by W. R. MacAskill, was first minted. Ever since, the Canadian 10¢ piece has had the image of a large fishing schooner on its obverse. Although a name does not appear, *Bluenose* is easily recognized, carrying full sail on two masts towering over her hull.

1938 found *Bluenose* restored to her former glory in full sail again. A challenge had come from Captain Benjamin Pine, still master of *Gertrude L. Thebaud*. He wanted to race for the International Fishermen's Trophy.

Now 17 years old, *Bluenose* had aged over the years. She had lost significant speed, and could not carry proper ballast for heavy going. Yet, she would answer the challenge. Her diesel engines were removed and she was again fitted with sails.

The schooners met off the New England shore. *Gertrude L. Thebaud* crossed the finish line two minutes, 56 seconds ahead of *Bluenose* in the first race.

Nova Scotians became uneasy at the mere thought of losing the cup. The provincial government summoned designer Bill Roué from his home in Dartmouth to go to New England to offer his assistance. It was a rushed trip for Roué and they even held the ferry in Yarmouth for his arrival.

On inspection, Roué found the defending champion to be five inches too long on the waterline. To make the proper adjustment, Captain Walters sent ashore about five tons of weight comprised of oil tanks, air tanks, and a lighting plant (generator). As a result, *Bluenose* handled noticeably better, and went on to capture the second and third races. *Thebaud* won the fourth.

With the score tied at two races each going into the last

race of this prolonged series, *Bluenose* outpaced *Thebaud* and won. She had remained undefeated in her quest for the International Fishermen's Trophy. Indeed, her brilliant racing and fishing career had earned *Bluenose* the title of Queen of the North Atlantic for all time.

A year later, the Second World War broke out in Europe, and attentions turned to more serious matters.

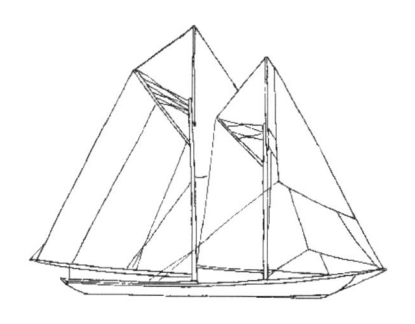

7. The War Years

Bill Roué was contacted by one of his neighbours, C. E. Pearce, Superintendent of the Harbour Ferry Commission, late in 1939. Pearce proposed that Bill design a new ferry, of timber construction and with three vehicle lanes, for service between Dartmouth and Halifax. Cars, trucks, horse-drawn wagons, and pedestrians were using the service at the time.

Bill agreed, and a tender was put out for the construction. The contract was awarded to Hugh Weagle of Dartmouth. The idea of a new ferry generated a wave of excitement locally; it would be both designed and built at home!

School children were asked to submit names for the new ferry. The name, *Governor Cornwallis*, was chosen.

On the day of the launching in 1941, school children were given a half holiday to commemorate the event. Approximately 5,000 people watched and cheered as *Governor Cornwallis* slipped into Halifax Harbour. Guests of honour included the premier of Nova Scotia, the mayor of Halifax, builder Hugh Weagle, and designer W. J. Roué.

Unfortunately, the vessel was ill-fated. A little more than

three years later, *Governor Cornwallis* caught fire. There were no injuries, but the ferry was a total loss.

For the first three years of the Second World War, *Bluenose* remained tied at a dock in Lunenburg, her birthplace. Still owned privately by the Bluenose Schooner Company, she was beginning to slip into debt, as money was still owed on the expensive diesel power plant installed, removed, and reinstalled. The owners could no longer afford the losses. The solution: *Bluenose* would have to be put up for auction.

Angus Walters, former captain, was dismayed. He was now operating a dairy business in Lunenburg, and pooled his resources to purchase controlling shares in the company. Captain Walters still believed in *Bluenose*, and thought it was disgraceful that the people she had so faithfully served would allow her fate to be decided in this manner.

Unfortunately, the captain's efforts only delayed the inevitable. In 1942, *Bluenose* was sold to the West Indies Trading Company. She was to be used for shipping freight such as sugar, rum, and coconuts in the southern waters of the Caribbean. Her towering masts were clipped, and powered by a diesel engine, she played out what were to be her final years.

During the war years, W. J. Roué designed a sectional barge of his own invention known as the Minca freight barge. It is believed to be the first sectional barge built anywhere in the world.

Roué designed his barge on the principle of a prefabricated house. The six sections could be transported overseas into the war zone on the deck of a ship, then assembled on site for landing troops and supplies as the Allies fought to open new fronts. Each barge was 50 ton, and capable of carrying a 100 ton load at a speed of four knots using a unique two and a half ton outboard motor. The barge could turn in its own length.

Once the plans were completed, Bill Roué was on the road constantly to five Maritime shipyards inspecting their construction. They were located at Mahone Bay, Parrsboro, and New Glasgow in Nova Scotia; and at Buctouche and Fredericton in New Brunswick. Now in his early 60s, Bill found the travel to be a severe strain on his health; but he regarded it as part of his war service. Quite often his son Jim would drive Roué around to complete the inspections.

All materials used in the barge, with the exception of the motor, were produced in Nova Scotia. The motors came from Sherbrooke, Québec. Due to wartime shortages, the rubber needed to go between the barge sections was unavailable. Bill discovered that harness felt made a perfect substitute. His improvisation allowed construction to continue. The first barge was launched in Mahone Bay, to undergo trials prior to being commissioned by the army.

Roué also designed tugs to pull the barges. Smith and Rhuland Shipyards in Lunenburg, and Industrial Shipping Company in Mahone Bay, constructed a total of 15 tugs.

These two projects created enormous economic benefits to the Maritimes during the difficult war years. The British Purchasing Commission for the war effort bought $29 million worth of the barges from the five Maritime shipyards, allowing the Mahone Bay site alone to put 300 men back to work.

In the middle of all this wartime activity, W. J. Roué moved his office from Barrington Street to Hollis Street, close to Province House, in downtown Halifax. The same year, 1944, at the request of the Armdale Yacht Club in Halifax, Bill Roué designed a class of small yachts, called the Bluenose Class, which would perpetuate the memory of the famed racer. It was Roué Plan #161, and not long after the end of the Second World War, 12 of these yachts were built.

Picture Section

Bluenose. Public Archives, Halifax, Nova Scotia

W. J. Roué circa 1920, when *Bluenose* was designed.
Maritime Museum of the Atlantic

W. J. Roué's gold watch, presented by the Town of Dartmouth, 1921.
Joan Roué

W. J. Roué at work, circa 1935. *Maritime Museum of the Atlantic*

W. J. Roué's home, 23 James Street, Dartmouth, Nova Scotia.
Joan Roué

W. J. and Winifred (Conrod) Roué, circa 1945. *Roué family*

P4

W. J. Roué (1879-1970), outside Dartmouth home, circa late 1960s. *Jim Roué*

James (Jim) Frederick Roué (1910-1991), W. J. Roué's eldest son, aboard *Bluenose II*, circa late 1980s. *E. Fraser Robinson*

Captain Wayne Walters, master of *Bluenose II* (grandson of Captain Angus Walters, master of *Bluenose*) with Lawrence (Laurie) James Roué (grandson of W. J. Roué, *Bluenose* designer) at *Bluenose II* recommissioning, May 28, 1995, Lunenburg, N.S. *Joan Roué*

Bluenose II, Halifax Harbour, 1984. *Al Kingsbury*

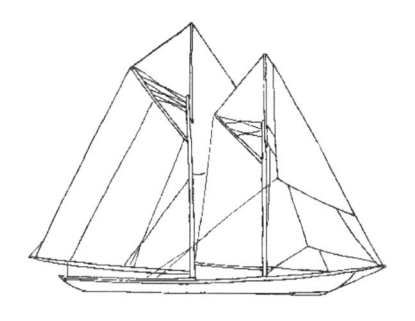

8. Bluenose Ghost

Many a heart was heavy when word reached shore that, on January 29, 1946, *Bluenose* had struck a coral reef off the coast of Haiti. The engines were salvaged the next day, and that night, she sank to her final resting place many fathoms below the surface.

Bluenose did not rest alone for long, however. Ironically, her most recent rival, *Gertrude L. Thebaud*, found her watery grave not far from *Bluenose* just a couple of years later.

It has never been fully explained how *Bluenose* found the extra knots which made the difference between victory and defeat. Opinions varied when old salts got together and talked of the performance of the famed racer.

However, there is one undisputed fact: *Bluenose* had speed. The following evidence is offered by Hugh F. Pullen, a retired rear admiral who was an officer aboard the Canadian destroyer, *Champlain,* which accompanied *Bluenose* to Gloucester in 1930. *Bluenose* was on her way to participate in the exhibition series with *Gertrude L. Thebaud* for the Sir Thomas Lipton trophy. During the voyage, Pullen's destroyer had to do "revolutions for 14 knots just to keep up with her." In other words, his vessel was working as hard as she could just to maintain the cruising speed of the sailing schooner, *Bluenose*.

It had been reported: "Her passing is a national sorrow; the disgrace of her death, a national shame." She had been the pride and joy of a small seagoing town on the South Shore of Nova Scotia. Lunenburg was still in mourning. "Why not build another *Bluenose*?" Many had asked this question after the original schooner was lost at sea that sad day in 1946.

Surely W. J. Roué also felt something deep within on the day that the news of *Bluenose*'s fate reached him. However, even though she had been his most illustrious design, she was, after all, only one of many in a long and distinguished career. His work continued and by 1948, Bill had moved his office to his home in Dartmouth where, at the age of 69, he did custom designs for private clients.

Boats and sailing were still Bill Roué's life, along with his family, which had now grown to include grandchildren. One of his personal traditions was to make special occasion dinners, with all of the trimmings, for the entire family to enjoy. He would prepare these meals himself, and had done so even before the sudden death of his wife, Winnifred, in February of 1954.

Later that year the Armdale Yacht Club honoured Bill Roué, and made him a life member.

In 1958, talk of building a second *Bluenose* became prominent in the town of Lunenburg. The 1960 Lunenburg launching of a *Bounty* replica for use in a Hollywood film, however, became the catalyst for serious *Bluenose II* possibilities. At the *Bounty* launching, there was an excitement in Lunenburg that had not been felt for many years. A very familiar, eery feeling — like that of a ghost — hovered about, as whispers of "It could be *Bluenose!*" swept through the air.

The *Bounty* seemed to prove that a *Bluenose* replica was possible. Construction estimates for a *Bluenose II* amounted to more than $200,000, and there would have to be minor alterations from the original plans to conform to new safety regulations. And of course, Lunenburg's Smith and Rhuland Shipyards would have to build her, just as they had built the original *Bluenose*. The Rhuland family was still running the yard. John and Fred Rhuland had taken over from their father, George.

Bluenose II would be used primarily to entertain tourists, who would pay a fee for their voyage, and help the vessel be self-supporting. This theory made perfect sense to excited Lunenburg citizens, especially as many tourists still looked for *Bluenose* when visiting their town. And Bill Roué agreed: *Bluenose* would be a good tourist attraction; Nova Scotians, and visitors alike, should have the opportunity to experience the schooner's magic.

But could they build another *Bluenose?* The design could be copied, but would she be as fast? No one really ever knew what had made her so swift: her design, that sloping hull, which, strangely, never left any dead water; her construction; her master, Captain Angus Walters? W. J. Roué thought another *Bluenose* right off his original plans might be as fast, or even faster, although, he always added, the original was special.

Everyone agreed this concept was a wonderful idea, but would it be practical? Would a new *Bluenose* race? Would she fish? Who would be in control of her operations? Most importantly, how would they finance her construction?

Although there were many proposals, the most popular was to launch a national campaign looking for the contributions of *Bluenose* dimes from Canadian school children. However, for one reason or another, this proposal, along with the others, failed. Hope of seeing another *Bluenose* diminished.

At the same time, Oland & Son, Limited, a Halifax brewery, was making plans to build its own schooner from *Bluenose* lines. They had even gone so far as to approach W. J. Roué about using the plans. Their vessel would be used as a publicity attraction to promote a new brand of beer, called Schooner. It would also serve as a private pleasure yacht for the owners. She would be named *Oland's Schooner*. However, when the brewery owners realized that the town of Lunenburg was launching its own campaign to resurrect the Queen of the North Atlantic, they dropped their plans.

Aware of the Oland's proposal, the Town of Lunenburg put together a delegation, headed by former captain Angus Walters. The group approached the firm to ask if Oland & Son, Limited would consider building a second *Bluenose*. The brewery agreed to go ahead with its plans, deciding its vessel would be the *Bluenose* replica instead of *Oland's Schooner*.

Much to the delight of the citizens of Lunenburg, Oland & Son, Limited announced in 1962 that the firm had commissioned the building of *Bluenose II*. This project would be a living tribute to Nova Scotian skills. She would be an exact replica of the original racing salt banker, and a brilliant memorial to Canada's greatest sea legend.

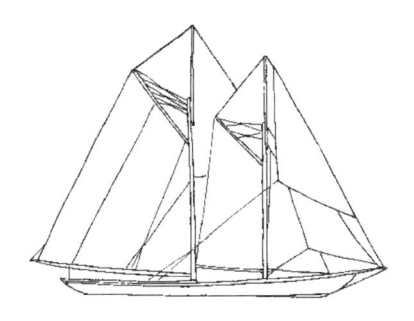

9. The Spirit Lives On

Bluenose II would still be used as a public relations tool for Oland's brewery, but she would be built, registered, maintained, and refitted out of Lunenburg. She would annually attend the Fisheries Exhibition in Lunenburg, and would be at the disposal of the fair's management during the event. *Bluenose II* would be a nonprofit making operation. All income earned by the schooner while at the fair would go to the fair's treasury. She would never be used as a freighter for her firm's products, nor would she ever race or fish. *Bluenose II* would be an honourable successor of a past glory, a tall-masted beauty with a bright, new mission.

Both Captain Walters and Bill Roué were consulted. Roué made his plans available, although interior alterations would be necessary to accommodate the pleasure yacht requirements of the owners.

A spokesman for Oland & Son, Limited said: "We may build and operate the schooner, but *Bluenose II* will always belong to the Canadians who loved the first vessel and applauded her achievements."

The keel for the new schooner was laid February 27, 1963, in a building shed at Smith and Rhuland Shipyards in Lunenburg. Captain Angus Walters, designer W. J. Roué, and Colonel Sidney Oland of Oland & Son, Limited, took turns driving the golden spike into her keel. Not 20 yards away, the Governor General of Canada had undertaken the same task on the original *Bluenose* in 1921.

Bluenose II would be a magnificent copy of her ancestor on the exterior. Below deck, however, would be very different: guest cabins and staterooms panelled in walnut, and a television equipped saloon, all furnished like a royal yacht. This would certainly be a far reach from the bunk-lined fo'c'sle cabins, forward of the fish holds, which the hands of the original vessel had experienced.

A few months later, in Halifax, on June 18, 1963, Bill Roué was honoured at a reception and dinner at the Royal Nova Scotia Yacht Squadron, North America's oldest yacht club, founded in 1837. He was 83, and the squadron's senior member, a life member, and past officer. When the club presented him with a silver trophy, Bill Roué in turn presented it to the club, as a perpetual challenge trophy.

Yachting people from the Halifax area, and representatives from civic and provincial governments attended the function. Many offered glowing testimonies to Bill Roué's contributions to yachting. Representing the Province of Nova Scotia, Mines Minister Donald Smith said Roué "had done more for yachting in Nova Scotia or Canada than any other single person in the history of Canadian yachting." Ex RNSYS commodore, Harvey Doane, called Bill Roué "one of the most enthusiastic yachtsmen in Canada. He is an inspiration to all who know him." City representative, Alderman Tom Trainor, said "Every time we flip a dime we think of yacht designer Bill Roué." A message from the president of the Canadian

Yachting Association termed Roué "a great honour to Canada." Telegrams from leading yacht designers in other parts of North America were also received and read at the dinner.

At that time, Roué was still working at his drawing board in his office at his home on James Street, high on the hill in Dartmouth, overlooking the harbour. Although the years had slowed him, he still insisted on completing each project personally. He had never remarried, and his family had expanded to include great-grandchildren by this time.

When July 23, 1963, rolled around, W. J. Roué knew where he had to be, as did thousands of people from all over the country. It was a day unlike any other in Lunenburg, Nova Scotia, as those gathered were to witness history in the making. For on the ways, at Smith and Rhuland Shipyards, lay ready *Bluenose II*, awaiting the command that would launch her.

Finally, she began to slide into the water, neither as a workhorse of the fishery nor as a racing vessel. The crowd of 6,000 cheered loudly as she plunged into Lunenburg Harbour, prepared to chart her own way into the pages of history. As she hit the water, the sun simultaneously burst forth from what had been an overcast sky.

At the launching ceremony of the $250,000 replica, Victor deB. Oland, president of Oland & Son, Limited, owners of *Bluenose II*, said: "A few years ago the citizens of Lunenburg took the decision to build a replica of *Bluenose*—a major difficulty was finance. Captain Angus Walters came to us and we were only too pleased to help. After all, *Bluenose* is one of the greatest symbols Canada ever had. We feel it will help Nova Scotia immensely, increasing the tourist traffic and advertising the province generally."

Although *Bluenose II* was a stately lady, she was expected

to earn her keep. Operated by the Olands, she would spend her summers in the waters off Atlantic Canada, or be berthed at either Halifax or Lunenburg, where visitors would be welcomed aboard. She could be chartered for cruises, and would often make a scheduled stop at Maritime ports. While in port, she could be seen and experienced as a proud memento of Nova Scotian and Canadian maritime heritage. During the winter months, she would sail south to the Caribbean waters, working as a charter ship, entertaining vacationers, and also illustrating Nova Scotia's prowess in shipbuilding.

Since the day she first sailed from her home port, on January 12, 1964, *Bluenose II* proved herself a worthy successor to her illustrious namesake. Her speed was inevitably compared to that of the original, and she too triumphed over Mother Nature's death dealing blows.

On her maiden voyage to the Island of Cocos, she fought for her life in a hurricane similar to the gale her predecessor had weathered in 1926. Beaten by the seas, and battered by 100 mph winds, she emerged victorious and intact.

During Canada's centennial year, in 1967, having hosted more than one million visitors, and logged more than 60,000 nautical miles, *Bluenose II* accepted the position as host ship at EXPO '67 in Montréal, Québec. So many visitors trampled her deck, it was worn thin. She returned to Halifax, then to Lunenburg, for her annual refit, including new deck planking, before charting her usual winter course to Antigua.

Bluenose II was now not only a sailing memorial to the original *Bluenose,* and the pride of all Nova Scotians, but was quickly and ably taking on the role of goodwill ambassador for Canada.

As *Bluenose II* was charting her way into history, her designer had grown ill. At 90 years of age, on January 14,

1970, William James Roué passed away at his home, in Dartmouth.

During his career, Bill Roué had designed over 200 vessels, and hundreds were built to his plans. From tugs to pilot boats, from ferries to yachts, and, of course sail boats, W. J. Roué had designed just about anything that would float. Although the fame of *Bluenose* overshadowed other vessels he designed, it's rather ironic to realize he was never even paid for that design.

Bill Roué was recognized as one of the best helmsmen in Canada, sailing numerous boats to victory himself. Many owners of his creations said the vessels were better yachts, than they were yachtsmen.

W. J. Roué's work was admired by his peers, including skilled American designers Starling Burgess, Phil Rhodes, and B. B. Crowninshield. Well-known journalist, author, and publisher, Jerry Snyder, who reported on every important sailing contest in America from 1898 until he (Snyder) died, said of his acquaintance, "Bill Roué is the greatest designer of wooden vessels Canada has ever produced."

Among W. J. Roué's clients were engineers, senators, Canadian federal, provincial, and municipal offices, the Government of the United Kingdom, and, yes, the every-day working man of modest means.

Bill Roué's friends were many, spread throughout Canada, Britain, and the United States. His skill was God-given, yet he remained a man in whom modesty and charm were outstanding characteristics. Many believed he had a gift—some thought typical of a genius. Bill Roué was said to be years ahead of his time with his very successful creations.

It has been stated that naval architects, particularly those doing yacht design, must be 75% artist and 25% engineer; and every design, no matter how large or small, must be an inspiration, and a labour of love. I wonder if they were describing my great-grandfather and his work when this remark was made.

William James Roué—loving family man, good friend, naval architect, yachtsman, and artist.

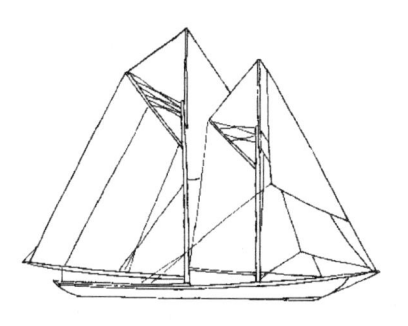

Epilogue

When *Bluenose II* had been constructed, she was "a gift, in trust, to the people of Nova Scotia." On September 7, 1971, her owner–builders, Oland & Son, Limited, of Halifax, sold the vessel to the Province of Nova Scotia for just one dollar. The government would now be in charge of maintaining and operating the schooner, beginning with an extensive refit she would need before she could set sail again.

In 1972, a Save the *Bluenose* campaign was launched to finance the $250,000 repair bill. School children all across Canada raised more than $155,000. The balance after public donations was covered by the provincial government.

The refit was successfully completed, and in 1974, *Bluenose II* set out as Nova Scotia's sailing ambassador for Norfolk, Virginia. She then worked her way up the eastern seaboard of the United States, visiting ports along the way.

In the spring of 1975, *Bluenose II* left on a six–week promotional tour of Canada's interior and the United States, through the St. Lawrence River and the Great Lakes. When she returned to Halifax, she settled into her new berth at the recently completed Historic Properties on the Halifax waterfront.

Bluenose II participated in the U.S. bicentennial celebrations of 1976. She made an extensive tour of American seaports, taking part in Operation Sail, a meeting of tall ships from around the world in New York City. The spring of 1978 saw *Bluenose II* heading south, first for Bermuda, then up the eastern seaboard of the United States, visiting 12 ports during the voyage.

Other memorable gatherings of tall ships took place in both Halifax and Sydney, Nova Scotia, as well as Québec City, Québec, in the summer of 1984. Each city hosted a breathtaking "Parade of Sail." *Bluenose II* was Canada's official host ship at all three sites.

Perhaps one of the most ambitious voyages she undertook began in 1985. *Bluenose II* departed on an 18-month, 18,000-mile journey to Vancouver, British Columbia, for EXPO '86. Before returning to Nova Scotia, she had visited Bermuda, Jamaica, Panama, Costa Rica, Acapulco, San Diego, Long Beach, San Francisco, Seattle, Victoria, Norfolk, New York City, and Boston.

The government of Canada again honoured *Bluenose II* and her predecessor, when Canada Post issued a commemorative stamp in 1988, featuring Angus Walters, captain of the original *Bluenose*. And in April of the same year, the Province of Nova Scotia issued its first license plates bearing the image of *Bluenose*. This unique, very distinguishable plate is still in use today.

In 1992, during Canada's 125th anniversary celebrations, Canada Post also presented a plaque to *Bluenose II*, in recognition of her role in promoting Canada around the world. This presentation took place in Québec City, aboard

Bluenose II during a St. Lawrence Seaway sail, when she also visited Toronto and Montréal.

From world expos to community festivals, *Bluenose II* had been an honoured guest, and both Canada's and Nova Scotia's goodwill ambassador, promoting tourism and industrial development, and reflecting Canada's proud maritime heritage. Throughout her lifetime, and as recently as 1993, *Bluenose II* had often participated in Nova Scotia's summer festivals and events. Public sailings and charters were offered to residents and visitors alike. Since her launching in 1963, *Bluenose II* had shared her decks with millions of people at ports in the Caribbean, on the St. Lawrence Seaway, in the Great Lakes, and up and down the coasts of North America. All those who had visited *Bluenose II*, or even only witnessed her as she sailed, had undoubtedly been touched by her magic, and impressed by her size: more than 180 feet in overall length and 125 feet high.

So it was a sad day indeed on March 17, 1994, when the Nova Scotia government announced that *Bluenose II* would sail no longer. She was reportedly unfit, and would need upwards of $1 million for repairs, funds the government could ill afford.

The announcement created quite a stir regarding the dilemma of *Bluenose II's* future, or the possibility of a *Bluenose III*. Immediately several private groups expressed interest in building a replica. Initially, only two groups actually mobilized publicly to take action.

The Bluenose Pride Seafaring Co-operative made plans to build a racing schooner along the lines of the original *Bluenose*, but using modern construction techniques. This group announced its venture in late March, 1994. The second organization, the Schooner Bluenose Foundation, was a non-political group, sanctioned by the Nova Scotia government. It announced on June 3, 1994, that its primary mandate was to launch a national fund raising campaign to ensure the building of *Bluenose III*. The foundation estimated it needed to raise $10 million, $7 million to build the vessel, and $3 million for operations.

The provincial government felt a *Bluenose* replica clearly enjoyed a special status as a fund raising cause. Results of a study undertaken by Nova Scotia's Economic Renewal Agency revealed:

1) The *Bluenose* was considered to be very important to Nova Scotia, both as promoting tourism and as a symbol of the province's heritage.

2) The *Bluenose* is among Nova Scotians' most cherished symbols of their province. There is virtual consensus among Nova Scotians that the *Bluenose* is one of the most important attractions that Nova Scotia has and it should continue to play this role.

3) The majority of Nova Scotians favour the construction of a new *Bluenose* schooner to repairing the existing one. The public is solidly behind the construction of a new vessel, and overall, seven in ten Nova Scotians favour the building of a new vessel. The building of this new vessel would be looked on as an opportunity to educate Canadians about their heritage and culture.

In spite of the government's survey, however, public opinion still varied regarding the fate and future of *Bluenose II*, or the building of a new replica. Controversy seemed to enter discussion on the subject everywhere. From the Nova Scotia government's point of view, however, only one thing seemed for sure: *Bluenose II* was finished. She would be towed between Lunenburg and Halifax to be a dockside tourist attraction.

This vision of *Bluenose II* got a lot of people's blood boiling. Imagine Nova Scotia's, perhaps even Canada's most recognizable, seafaring symbol at the end of a rope. How could this be? To add insult to injury, rumoured long term plans were to strip her of her hardware, tow her out to sea, and sink her!

Meanwhile, in Lunenburg County, the Bluenose Pride group was selling shares in its venture much the same way the Bluenose Schooner Company had done in 1921 for *Bluenose*. In 1994, however, they needed to raise $8 million, as compared to $35,000 for the original schooner.

The Schooner Bluenose Foundation had not yet made any public pleas for funds, but had commenced advertising for fund raising proposals and for a vessel construction manager.

Enter Halifax lawyer Wilfred Moore, aggravated about the fate of *Bluenose II*; so aggravated in fact, that on September 28, 1994, he announced plans to save her. He had established, with the blessing of the provincial government, the Bluenose II Preservation Trust. The new non–profit group had a deadline, however—June, 1995, when the leaders of the world's most powerful industrial democracies would be gathering for the annual G–7 summit, in Halifax, June 15-17.

Bluenose II would be expected to take part in the event, according to newspaper reports of late August, 1994. Canadian Prime Minister, Jean Chrétien, had been behind a request to have her available to the G-7 leaders during their Halifax visit. The summit's 1995 location, and the prime minister's request had combined to help save *Bluenose II*, perhaps making the Halifax summit the most fortuitous event of her life.

Moore and his committee put the restoration job out for public tender. Snyder's Shipyard Ltd., headed by Philip Snyder, was awarded the contract. The tender stated the vessel was to be brought back to Class One Certification, a four–year term status granted by the Canadian Coast Guard, following rigorous inspections. The estimate for the full refit was $500,000. Funding for the restoration would come from the federal and provincial governments, and the private sector.

Bluenose II was hauled up in Lunenburg, on January 4, 1995. The first cut was made in her hull on January 12th.

As in the story of her initial building, and that of her predecessor, Nova Scotian materials were used where possible. All of the new wood came from New Germany, a small Lunenburg County community inland from the town of Lunenburg. The three tons of spikes used to secure the timbers were made in Dartmouth, home of W. J. Roué. The 45–man crew was composed of skilled local craftsmen, determined to "do the job right."

According to Philip Snyder, master boat builder, close to 80% of the planking on her hull was replaced, as was over 60% of her framing. Twenty-one thousand board feet of spruce and 24,000 board feet of hardwood were used on the job.

Each piece had to be removed in sections so that a pattern could be made. A new plank, about 20 feet long, had to be hand planed to fit the old pattern, and then steamed for about an hour and a half. Up to six men then had to carry the steaming hot plank to the vessel, and place it in the correct position. Once the planking was completed, the spaces between the boards were filled with several layers of cotton and oakum, then sealed with a special type of cement. The final steps included sanding, finishing, and painting.

Below decks, the crew from Snyder's Shipyard Ltd. went

to work on remodelling *Bluenose II's* ventilation system. A poor one at the best of times, the system had been a major contributor to the rotting problem encountered during her refit.

Having worked on boats for more than 56 years, Philip Snyder estimates *Bluenose II* will be seaworthy for at least another eight to ten years, emphasizing this was not a patch-up job. During the refit, an inspector from the Canadian Coast Guard made regular examinations. In addition, although the Class One license is a four-year term, *Bluenose II* will be inspected every year as a prerequisite to receiving her annual safety certificate.

Captain Wayne Walters, of Lunenburg, is at the helm of *Bluenose II*, commanding a roster of Nova Scotian officers and crew chosen from dozens of applicants for the 1995 season. The appointment of Walters is significant, both historically and practically: Walters is the grandson of Angus Walters, original captain of *Bluenose*, and the only Canadian qualified to take *Bluenose II* into foreign ports; he alone holds a master mariner foreign–going certificate for fore and aft sailing vessels.

Other Nova Scotians who will sail *Bluenose II* and who will help Captain Walters restore the magic of Canada's sailing ambassador include: Delbé Comeau of Meteghan River, chief officer; B. Eric England of Maders Cove, chief engineer; and Andrew J. Caldwell of Centreville, second officer.

Of the original $500,000 refit estimate, the contract came in under budget at $418,000. The Province of Nova Scotia agreed to pay $90,000, the Canadian government agreed to pay $210,000, and the rest would come from the private sector.

With the refit completed, Wilfred Moore said *Bluenose II*

could sail beyond the year 2000, and he fully expects her to be leading the Tall Ship Parade of Sail to be held in Halifax Harbour in that year. Her day to day operations will be administered by the Bluenose II Preservation Trust committee, with Moore as chair. He believes "she is a national treasure," and admires the vessel more for her historical significance and craftsmanship, than for her public relations value.

In 1995, *Bluenose II* will stay close to home, to allow her people plenty of opportunity to experience her again. And as in the past, *Bluenose II* will be available for public cruises as well as private charters. She has already been booked for three weddings in the summer of '95.

The Bluenose II Preservation Trust also announced it intends to make available three berths for training purposes. Two will be offered to the Nautical Institute in Cape Breton, and one to the Canadian Navy.

Nova Scotians will be asked to donate to a maintenance fund to keep *Bluenose II* sailing for many years to come. The Province of Nova Scotia will retain ownership of the vessel, and will continue to pay her annual operating costs until such time as the trust can do so.

The Bluenose Pride Seafaring Co—operative continues to attract funds for its venture. The group has not, to date, debuted final plans for its vessel, although it has stated, "based closely on William Roué's brilliant lines for the original Bluenose, but taking advantage of all appropriate techniques in engineering and design, *Bluenose Pride* will be strong, easy to maintain and very, very fast."

And still there are the critics who seem to be willing to toss aside this piece of our maritime heritage. Perhaps they should weigh their resolution against the fact that hundreds of thousands of people still rush to catch a glimpse of this elegant schooner; that *Bluenose II* has generated both boundless pride and untold revenues for Nova Scotians and Canadians alike.

But for now, even the Nova Scotia government has taken a firm stand on the issue. On April 3, 1995, the province publicly acknowledged the restoration of *Bluenose II*, stating, "She will sail forever." According to Robbie Harrison, Minister of Nova Scotia's Economic Renewal Agency, which is responsible for *Bluenose II*, "The *Bluenose* legacy has come to mean a great deal to the Province of Nova Scotia, and indeed to Nova Scotians themselves. Therefore, we are pleased that *Bluenose II* will be sailing again this summer. As always, *Bluenose II* will be a magnificent ambassador for Nova Scotia, when international attention will focus on us during the Halifax Summit this June." Mr. Harrison went on to state that, "For the time being, fund raising for *Bluenose III* has been placed on hold until the long-term future of *Bluenose II* is determined."

On May 8, 1995, at around 2:20 PM, *Bluenose II* was finally returned to the salt water she loves so dearly. Because much work remained to be done topside, including recommissioning her engines, she was towed from her Lunenburg cradle back to her berth, alongside the Lunenburg Fisheries Museum.

Although it was a nasty, dreary day, a good-sized crowd showed up to witness a miracle in the making—just a year ago she was doomed; now she was back in the water again, looking as proud and beautiful as ever. A stirring sight indeed! And as an omen perhaps, just as she touched the dock, the sun peeped out from behind the clouds and shone through the mist, welcoming *Bluenose II* back home.

So for now "*Bluenose* is Sailing Once Again."

My Opinion

I believe, as I am sure would my great-grandfather W. J. Roué, that a *Bluenose* legacy needs to remain always. In the future, when required, a true replica of *Bluenose* should be built, both to educate and remind people of a very important connection to our past, while remembering the risks taken, the challenges met, and the victories won—setting an example for the world today.

It is important to remember that the illustrious *Bluenose*, undisputed Queen of the North Atlantic, was built to demonstrate Canadian prowess in fishing and seamanship. She did not disappoint. Her place in history was won as she became a famous racing fisherman schooner, not only successful in taking on all comers in international racing competition, but also surviving and working in the worst weather the North Atlantic could dish out.

Bluenose was a full-time fishing schooner, working the Grand Banks with many other vessels, reaping their harvest for the fish markets of the world. This grand Lunenburg salt banker established a record for the largest single catch of fish landed in Lunenburg during the 1920s. She was one of the world's best known wind ships; she became a legend. *Bluenose* captured the attention of prime ministers, monarchs, and presidents throughout the world. The name *Bluenose* was known and honoured.

Many were the exploits of the original *Bluenose*. Her greatest triumph is the legacy she left us. Her design has been studied and imitated many times; her success never duplicated. Her appeal is mysteriously similar to the calling of the sea, or the flames of a fire. We should not ever even consider casting aside this heritage.

Postscript

May 28, 1995, was a very special Sunday. That afternoon, during a public recommissioning ceremony at the Lunenburg Fisheries Museum in Lunenburg, Nova Scotia, *Bluenose II* was placed back into service after more than a year on the sidelines.

The vessel sat ever so proudly alongside, gaily decorated and ready for the festivities. As the hour approached, the crowd swelled until there were more than 1000 people jammed on the dock.

The Town Crier read his script and rang his bell, signalling the start of the ceremony. Speeches were given, acknowledgements were made, and Philip Snyder, head of Snyder's Shipyard Ltd., the shipwrights who had completed the restoration, handed over *Bluenose II's* key to Nova Scotia's premier, John Savage

Bluenose II Preservation Trust chairman, Wilfred Moore, called upon Derek Wells, Member of Parliament for the South Shore, to make a special presentation on behalf of the Government of Canada to Wayne Walters, the captain of *Bluenose II*.

Mr. Wells unfurled a large Canadian flag, explaining to Captain Walters that this flag, now to fly from *Bluenose II*, had flown on the Peace Tower in Ottawa, Canada's capital, until April 27, 1995. It had been removed that day in recognition of the 116th anniversary of the birth of William James Roué, designer of the *Bluenose*.

I, for one, will remember W. J. Roué whenever I see that particular flag flying over the spectacular vessel he created. I will always feel a sense of familial pride, but also a renewed pride, and deep appreciation for a group of Nova Scotians, led by Wilfred Moore of Halifax, who were able to breathe life back into *Bluenose II* when she was all but doomed.

Meanwhile, the new flag flying above the recommissioned vessel will sail with her wherever she may venture—always a reminder to *Bluenose II* that the spirit of W. J. Roué is still looking over her.

PART 2

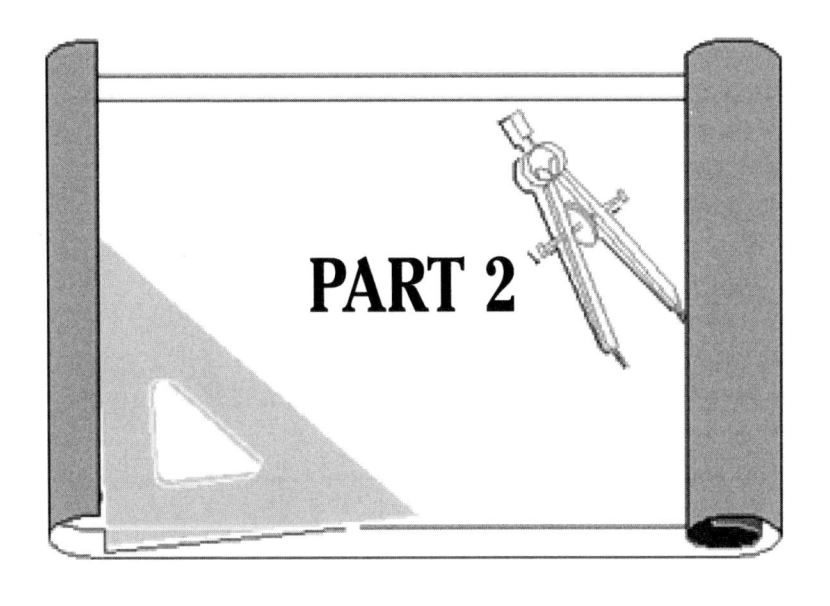

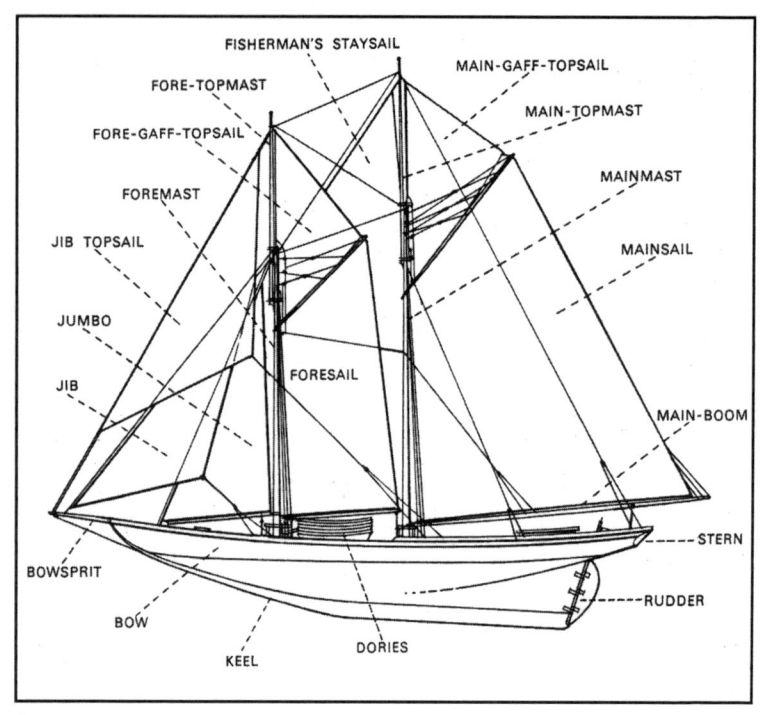

Diagram of schooner.

The following article appeared in the *Halifax Herald*, Dec. 30, 1923. It is reprinted with the permission of The Halifax Herald Ltd.

How Bluenose Was Designed
By W. J. Roué

In this noteworthy article the genius who designed the world famous fishing schooner "Bluenose," tells how that ship was designed. Mr. Roué goes back to earliest days in schooner building and traces the development of that type of vessel. His remarks on the difference between Gloucester and Nova Scotia types and the necessity for stringent racing rules will interest many. So far as possible the writer has avoided technical terms and with those used the majority of Maritime readers will be familiar.

A schooner is a fore and aft rigged vessel. A topsail schooner has yards on her fore mast and sometimes on her main–mast, but no courses.

It is claimed that the name "schooner" originated in America in 1713 in this way, – Andrew Robinson (probably a Scotchman) built a vessel at Gloucester, Mass. At the launching as the vessel took the water a spectator was heard to remark, "How she scons." Robinson on hearing this said, "A Scooner let her be." Webster in his dictionary says that story is well authenticated and eight years later Moses Princes referred to Robinson as the "first contriver of schooners." Webster says the man said "how she scons" because the Scotch word scon is to skim as a flat stone will when thrown upon the water. It was just as probable that the name 'schooner' was derived from the Dutch 'schoone' pronounced 'schoona' meaning – clean, elegant, fair, beautiful, etc. Webster without giving any authority says that the German "schooner" the Danish "skooner" and the Spanish "escuna" were derived from the English or from the Scotchman who built the "schooner" in Gloucester, Mass. It is possible that the term was used before Robinson used it, but he is generally given credit as applied to vessels of two masts, both of which are fore and aft rigged.

The fishing vessels of Nova Scotia thirty years ago were deeper and of less breadth than those of fifteen years later. It was found that the deep narrow vessel required a large amount of permanent ballast, thereby cutting down carrying capacity and were not suitable for freighting trips in the winter months, and not easy to dispose of as coasters when their life as a fisherman was over.

They also sailed at a rank angle of heel, making living aboard anything but pleasant. A later development produced vessels of the "Delawanna" type. These vessels with their short over–hang forward and moderate depth were fast off the wind, fair to windward, good all round vessels for fishing as carried on in Nova Scotia.

The next type was the knock–about. Vessels of this type should have proved very efficient for our fishing, as every one is bound to acknowledge that a vessel without a bowsprit is a much better one to ride at anchor than a bowsprit vessel. But the type of broad flat hull of great natural stability, requires more sail than can be put on a vessel without having too high a rig, which is not good practice with inside ballasted vessels. Besides vessels of this type are generally hard to steer as the centre of effort is as a rule too far aft making the vessel in some cases round up in the wind in spite of the rudder being across the boat's course. Of course this could be obviated by having the centre of lateral resistance relatively far aft. This, however, might make her too light headed so that she would be inclined to have the bow knocked off to leeward when beating to windward in a heavy head sea.

It appears that the early Gloucester vessel was not a desirable type. Almost any of the older captains out of Gloucester will tell you that since the introduction of the Burgess type of vessel they have had no losses through stress of weather. The inference is that before the Burgess type they had sustained loss other than fire and running aground. Edward Burgess was no doubt the originator of the present day type of Gloucesterman.

The radical differences between the Nova Scotia vessel and the Gloucesterman is that the Gloucester vessels that are built for sailing only, are somewhat narrower and deeper, carrying a great amount of permanent ballast. They are used for fishing the entire year and a great majority fish under sail; that is, the vessel jogs while the dories are away fishing, sailing around and picking them up at nightfall.

The Gloucester vessels are much lower in freeboard than the Nova Scotia vessels, consequently very wet in rough water. They are better sailers to windward than our vessels are as a whole, but in strong breezes are no faster off the wind, if as fast. The Gloucester vessel being built of white oak and southern pitch pine have a much longer life than our vessels, but they are at the best no stronger in construction, better built or rigged.

The International Race

In the early Fall of 1920, W.H. Dennis was inspired with the idea that it would be a good thing for the fishing industry of this province to have a race between vessels of the salt banking fleet. Acting upon that inspiration he put up The Herald and Mail Trophy for the Championship of the Nova Scotia Fishing Fleet. Eight vessels competed and the Race, Cup and

Championship were won by the schooner "Delawanna," an eight-year old vessel, over the latest Knockabouts. This proved that the design of the fishing vessels out of Lunenburg and LaHave had not improved as far as speed was concerned in the preceding eight years. Shortly afterward The Herald and Mail International Fisherman's Trophy was put up for competition between fishing vessels of the Atlantic. Gloucester responded with the "Esperanto." Our defeat at the hands of that ill-fated vessel is still fresh in our memory. The Delawanna did very well off the wind, but could do nothing beating to windward against this type of vessel, so the cup was carried to Gloucester.

The Bluenose
After the defeat of the Delawanna by the Esperanto it was felt that we had no vessel of the Esperanto type on the wind. It was decided that if we ever hoped to have a fighting chance, something new and different would have to be built. When the order was given me for the design, it was clearly pointed out that the new vessel must have all the carrying capacity of the largest Knockabouts and have the smallest amount of permanent ballast consistent with safety. In fact the vessel would have to be a paying proposition either fishing or freighting.

Having the figures before me as to the weight of fish or freight that the vessel was expected to carry, the weight of hull, spars, sails, rigging and stores, it was found that at normal water line of 110 feet, 270 long tons of displacement was required. The next thing was to work out the proper distribution of displacement so as to cause the least resistance. It is known that a certain ratio of increasing progression of under-water bulk to the point of greatest transverse area at about 55 per cent of the water line length aft of the stem and decreasing bulk from that point aft causes the least resistance to bodies moving through the water at the surface. This is called the "wave form theory" and all modern yachts adhere closely to it. The theory is that the water excavated by the fore body of a vessel when she is moved through a fluid is carried away to infinity (not the actual particles, but a corresponding bulk), by a solitary carrier–wave, or wave of translation; and that the cavity formed by the greatest cross section as the body moves ahead is filled up by a wave of second order, or the common oscillating wave of the ocean. Therefore, the fore body should be shaped in length and distribution of displacement to correspond to the form of a carrier wave of equal length, or a curve of versed sines; the run or after body to the length and shape of the front of an oscillating wave or trochord. If so informed, the ship will meet with the least resistance in her progress. The Bluenose is designated to conform to this theory; in other ways she is a combination of the Gloucester and Nova Scotian vessels, having the depth of the former and the breadth of the latter.

This combination has worked out happily as she has proven herself to be at least as fast as any Nova Scotian vessel off the wind, and faster than any Gloucesterman that she has met on the wind. Captain Walters tells me that she is the driest vessel at anchor or under sail that he has ever sailed on.

Special Features in Bluenose Design
The Bluenose has demonstrated that vessels can be built having the breadth and carrying capacity of the Nova Scotian vessels; the depth and windward qualities of the Gloucesterman and still be reasonably fast. The outcome of the races (with sane rules to govern) will be the production of vessels of great speed and sea going ability, vessels that will make the name of Nova Scotia what it was in former years in

the maritime world when our ships were known in all ports of the world. Be it known that inside ballasted vessels have not been designed or built to sail in competition with one another since the advent of outside ballast of yachts; therefore the chance for improvement is great.

Reasons For Racing Rules
No one would expect an automobile of 2000 pounds weight and 50 horse power to compete with one of the same horse power and 500 pounds less weight. It must never be supposed that the intention of the donor of the trophy was to encourage the building of the fastest vessels within a given length and limit of sail area. The idea is to produce better and safer fishing vessels, faster if possible, with the same bulk or displacement as is usual practice. It would not be very hard for any designer to make a vessel of say 110 feet water line, 220 tons of displacement and 10,000 square feet of sail, faster than one of the same length and sail area but of 280 tons displacement; and the safety of vessels at sea is mainly due to a fair proportion of displacement to water line lengths coupled with good breadth and freeboard. These features also produce just what we want for our fishing vessels.

That limit of sail area of 80 per cent water line length, squared, was arrived at only after extensive research into sail areas of well–known sea–going vessels with inside ballast. The displacement rule was made to prevent the building of very light displacement, which would be totally unsuited to the fishing industry and not safe. After consultation with some of the foremost designers the following displacement rule was adopted by the trustees; that the cube root of the displacement in long tons must never be less than 5.8 per cent of the measured line; this is a compromise between the Nova Scotia and Gloucester types. It may be a surprise to many to know that the modern racing schooner yacht has a larger ratio of displacement to water than this limitation provides. It has been clearly shown during the short time these races have been held that the spars are in some cases getting too high, so for safety to the crews a limit has been put on them and as a fair amount of breadth is to be encouraged, it is used as a factor in obtaining the height limit. Thus, the following rule has been introduced by the trustees; that the height from deck to main–top–sail halyard block band shall never be more than the sum of one–half the water line length plus twice the greatest water line breadth plus the constant of 10.

The Specifications of *Bluenose*

Following are the specifications of the original *Bluenose* as initially set forth by designer W. J. Roué. This document was discovered recently amongst my great-grandfather's files. The original is presented typewritten on legal size paper, backed with a blue cover. Every effort has been made to present the details here as they appear in the original document.

NO. 17

SPECIFICATION
of
110 FOOT L.W.L. FISHING SCHOONER
Designed by
Wm. J. Roué
–:– –:–

DIMENSIONS:
Length O. A. about—141 feet 0 inches
Length W. L.—110 feet 0 inches
Breadth, extreme— 27 feet 0 inches
Breadth, l. w. l.— 26 feet 6 inches
Draught, extreme— 15 feet 6 inches

GENERAL DESCRIPTION:–
To be constructed generally as shown in the accompanying plans. The vessel is to be laid down to the outside of plank and plank is to be taken off in the mold loft.

IT SHALL BE EXPRESSLY UNDERSTOOD AND AGREED, That the work of every kind in and about the vessel shall be complete in all its various parts and details, and that the materials and workmanship needed to make the hull, with its fittings and fastenings, riveting, caulking, watertight work, ready for actual service, and built in accordance with the drawings attached hereto and under the direction of the owners or their representative, shall be furnished by the builder; and that if a description of any part or detail necessary to make the vessel complete and substantial may have been omitted from the following specification or from the drawings, such part or details shall be deemed part and parcel of the contract, and shall be furnished by the builder. It is the intent of these Specifications to describe the materials, construction and workmanship of the highest grade and most approved practice for this type of vessel, both in the hull, its fittings and all materials and workmanship required for the completion of the vessel in accordance with this intent shall be furnished and fitted by the builder, whether hereinafter specified or not.

The Designer's object is that these specifications and the plans shall be followed in every particular, but should it be necessary or advisable in the course of construction to make any changes in the arrangement or details of hull, joinery or other work, so long as the general style and character of the vessel maintained, such changes are to be made by the builder without extra compensation. Any portion of the work found defective, whether partially or entirely completed, must be removed and satisfactorily replaced by the builder at once, and without extra charge.

<u>MATERIAL and WORKMANSHIP</u>:

To be of the very best description and quality: the greatest care is to be exercised in having the Hull, rails, etc., perfectly eye sweet and fair. All to the satisfaction of the owners and their representative.

<u>KEEL</u>:

Keel to be of Birch to be sided 12 inches at rabbet, tapered to 10 inches at bottom, moulded as shown in profile drawing. Keel to be built up of as long lengths as possible to obtain. Scarfs to be well shifted, no scarf to come in way of masts, and all parts to be securely bolted together with galvanized bolts riveted over galvanized iron rings.

STEM:

Stem to be of Birch sided 12 inches at keel, tapered to 10 inches at deck. Moulded as shown and to be built up of natural curved timber, in long lengths and securely bolted to keel and at scarfs with galvanized iron bolts, riveted up over galvanized iron rings.

STERNPOST:

Sternpost to be Birch sided 12 inches at Horn, timber tapered to 6 inches at keel. Auxiliary sternpost to be sided 12 inches tapered to fair line of Rabbet.

DEADWOOD:

To be of Birch, sided as shown, and secured to keel and sternpost with galvanized iron bolts.

RUDDER:

Stock to be of Oak 12 inches at head and tapered to 6 inches at bottom. Blade to be securely bolted to stock with galvanized iron bolts. Blade to be tapered at after edge as shown on plan.

FRAME:

Double, sided 9 inches moulded 9 inches at keel and 6 inches at head to show 10 inches depth between keel and keelsons. To be spaced 27 inches centre to centre. Frame forward of Station No. 4 and aft of Station No. 12 to be sided 8 inches. Stations to be of well seasoned oak.

FLOORS:

Have same siding as frame, to be worked forward and aft of over keelson where frames are bolted to side of keel.

KEELSONS:

To be of Birch sided 12 inches moulded 20 inches deep, to be in as long lengths as possible, having no scarf in way of masts. To be securely bolted to frames and keel with heavy galvanized bolts riveted over galvanized rings.

PLANKING:

Birch or other approved hardwood, Garboards 4 inches thick, securely edge bolted to keel as well as frames. Second streak to be of sufficient thickness to allow fairing to 3 inch planking. Topsides to be 3 1/2 inches thick; to be of white or grey Oak.

Planks to be in as long lengths as possible. No adjoining streak to have butts less than four frame spaces apart and bolts coming in the same frame space to be separated by not less than five streaks.

Planks to be secured to frames with treenails and galvanized iron bolts.

All seams to be caulked under the direction and to the complete satisfaction of Captain Angus Walters.

CLAMPS:

To have heavy ceiling from deck to turn off bilge into bottom, to act as clamp streaks, to be of 5 inch Spruce in as long lengths as possible to obtain securely bolted through frames and planking, with galvanized iron bolts rivetted over rings.

SHELF STREAKS:

To be Spruce 5" x 7" tapered at ends to three streaks to be in as long lengths as possible. All butts well shifted and securely bolted to frame. Planks and deck beams with galvanized iron bolts rivetted over galvanized iron rings.

BILGE STREAKS:
To have three streaks on each side 5" x 10", Spruce, securely bolted to frame and plank with galvanized iron bolts over galvanized iron rings.

DECK BEAMS:
To be of best quality Oak sided 9 inches moulded 10 inches at centre and 8 inches at ends, to be securely fastened with galvanized iron bolts to shelf and frame end spaced according to hatch and house openings.

KNEES: HANGING KNEES:
One pair at Windlass, two pairs at foremast, two pairs at Main Hatch. On pair at break Beam, one pair at Main Mast, two pairs at After Hatch, one pair at Fore end of House, one pair at aft of House. Knees to extend well out on deck beams and down sides of vessel.
Lodging Knees as required.

WATER WAYS:
To be of 4 inch hardwood securely bolted to beams and Shelf with galvanized iron bolts rivetted over galvanized rings.

DECK:
Planking of 2 3/4 inch Pine clear and well seasoned. To be laid so that the grain of the wood will show.

CEILING:
To be of best quality Spruce, 3 inches thick, in as long lengths as possible, butts well shifted, securely fastened with treenails and galvanized bolts, to frame and planking. Ceiling in way of permanent ballast; to be left off until ballast is mould and cement set.

FASTENINGS:
To be of the best quality wood tree nails and galvanized bolts. No black iron to be used in any part of vessel. Tree nail to be sawed off on plank and ceiling and wedged at both ends. Every sixth fastening to be a through fastening of galvanized iron bolts.

DECK HOUSE:
To be built in usual manner for vessels of this type and arranged according to usual practice, and wishes of Captain Angus Walters.

SPARS:
Masts, topmast, main boom and bow-sprit to be of material and dimensions as shown in sail plan.

All iron work necessary for a vessel of this kind to be supplied and fitted by the Builder to the complete satisfaction of the owners or their representative.

PAINTING and FINISHING
The Hull to be planed and smoothed with sand paper, primed and given three coats of paint of an approved color above the water line, and two coats of copper paint below water line.

Deck to be painted with a good quality of deck paint and Deck House Hatch Ceamings (coamings) and Companion Ways to be painted White.

Rail to be of Oak and finished with Spar varnish.

FINAL CLAUSES:
The Builder to supply and install all necessary blocks, Mast hoops, storm sails, blaying (belaying) pins, complete all iron work, ventilators, four port lights to open in cabin, an additional port in toilet. Cabin to be finished in Oak varnish. Toilet supplied and installed in toilet room. Cabin and

forecastle to have hard wood floors and finished under Capt. Walters direction and instruction.

Builders to supply and install all fishing gear about decks, such as dory cradles, fish boxes, bait boards, water butts and stands, chain boxes, rail boxes, booby hatches, to large galvanized iron screw deck plates. One smaller size over potato lockers. Main boom irons to be fitted for two sets of chains boom tackles, etc. Salt to be put in vessel as instructed by Capt. Angus Walters.

Builders to do all carving and gilding of scroll work and name and furnish and gild topmast balls, etc.

All seams to be filled with material that can be planed and sand papered to the satisfaction of Capt. Angus Walters.

BALLASTING and CEMENTING

The owner shall supply 50 tons of boiler punching and builder put in the same mixed with Portland cement and sand between frames, keel and keelson, leaving as large a quantity of iron as possible in the mixture.

The Builder shall endeavor to keep all iron as low as possible and in the middle third of the vessel.

Steering gear and wheel to be supplied and fitted by Builder, windlass pattern approved by the owners, to be fitted and supplied by Builder. Also bronze hawse pipes and all other and sundry articles to make vessel ready for sea.

The Roué 20

The Roué 20 Class takes its name from W. J. Roué's Plan # 20. Originally the Star Class, Bill Roué designed this small sailboat in 1922.

The Roué 20 is quite basic, a very forgiving yacht, with fine, easy handling characteristics, and capable of sailing in most wind conditions. It has always been very highly regarded as an excellent racer.

Roué 20s were first built in the 1920s, again after the Second World War in the '50s, and then in the '70s, '80s, and even into the '90s. Originally wood, the Roué 20's most significant change since the '70 has been in construction materials. Now generally fibreglass over a wood core, the yachts are more durable.

The earlier models were gaff rigged, the later models marconi rigged. The sail area is approximately 450 square feet, and the keel consists of 2000 lbs. of lead. The vessels are 28 feet long overall, and 20 feet on the water.

During the early years of this one-design class, regular competitions took place in Halifax-Dartmouth waters. Apparently all Roué 20s had claimed a race except one. Puzzled, yet confident that this vessel too could win, Bill Roué took the helm himself and sailed her to victory at last.

The Roué 20 has maintained its popularity because of good handling characteristics and low cost. Being narrow beamed, with a deep fin and relatively long keel, the Roué 20 is an easy boat to handle for her size. She is also a functional yacht, sleeping four people comfortably in the cabin. Approximately 30 Roué 20s are estimated to be sailing in Atlantic Canadian waters today.

The Bluenose Class

The Bluenose Class is a one–design class of competitive sailboats. They were designed in 1944 by W. J. Roué, at the request of the Armdale Yacht Club.

Only five years after the first vessels set sail, the class was honoured by the *Halifax Herald* newspaper in Halifax, Nova Scotia. The following article introduced the International Bluenose Class Trophy. A perpetual trophy, the winning crew each year received a replica suitably engraved. The article appeared in the *Halifax Herald* on Tuesday, August 16, 1949, and is reproduced in part, with permission of The Halifax Herald Ltd.:

> To perpetuate the name and fame of a great champion, a Bluenose Class of yachts was started in this province in the period immediately following the close of the Second World War.
>
> The boats of the one–design class have spread far beyond the borders of Nova Scotia and have become, already, an international institution.
>
> These sturdy, honest little yachts with a smart turn of speed are from the board of W. J. Roué the Halifax naval architect who designed the Bluenose herself. At this date close on to 50 Bluenose Class yachts are racing in various parts of this country and the United States.
>
> The Bluenoses are a strong 23 feet overall and 16 feet on the water. They are "real" little yachts, carrying a substantial amount of lead keel, and with just about everything a modern yacht should have, including "Genoa" jibs and "parachute" spinnakers.
>
> This year, as the Halifax Bicentenary feature, the International Bluenose Race was inaugurated, and

hereafter the annual Bluenose International series will be raced in Halifax waters. The 1949 winner was a crew from Marblehead, Massachusetts.

These newspapers are glad, and feel honoured, to be associated with this International classic which will keep alive the memory of the greatest fishing schooner ever to swing canvas in Atlantic waters. It was the privilege of these newspapers to donate the trophies for which the original Bluenose raced and which she held throughout her entire career; and this International Bluenose Class Championship Trophy is in the true Bluenose tradition, as will be the contests of which it will be emblematic in the years to come.

Today, the Bluenose Class is still going strong, with more than 300 known to be sailing. This fine little vessel is especially popular in the Maritime Provinces, and in Southern Ontario, although they also sail in the United States.

About one quarter of these sailboats have wooden hulls, the rest are fibreglass. Most of the fibreglass–hulled ships are in Ontario, while Maritimers prefer the wooden hulls. The greatest number of these boats are built to Roué's original plans.

Bluenose Class President, Al Chaddock, of Halifax, feels that if W. J. Roué's specifications had been honoured over the years, there would be even more boats around today. Cutting costs in production has shortened the longevity of the boats. Mr. Chaddock also describes a Bluenose Class boat as "beautiful to sail, quick to accelerate—wonderful." The boats are still being built in various locations today.

Many are faithful supporters of the class. A Bluenose Class boat is fit for going out for a day sail, but most exciting in class races. Strict rules have kept the class competitive. It is interesting to note that a fibreglass hull has never won a class championship. The design is very friendly to the beginner, and inexpensive to maintain. Here is yet another fine example of a W. J. Roué-designed, Nova Scotian-built product which has stood the test of time.

What Is A Bluenose?

Although the name has been used since the early 1800s to describe natives of the province of Nova Scotia, the term's origin has never been absolutely resolved.

Dictionaries define bluenose as a nickname for a native or inhabitant of Nova Scotia, and Judge Thomas Haliburton, of Windsor, Nova Scotia, is given credit for making the term widely known outside the province through his writings which became popular more than a century ago. Haliburton is often suggested to have originated the term which first appeared in his works. He is considered by some to be the father of North American humour.

There are at least three different speculations as to how bluenose came to mean a native of Nova Scotia. Some believe it referred to a blue tinted potato called a bluenose grown by many Nova Scotians. Others say the name developed because Nova Scotia fishermen bound for the Grand Banks painted the bows, or noses, of their schooners a bright blue. Still others suggest it was the blue noses of Nova Scotians, exposed to the harsh Atlantic waters, which prompted the origin of the expression.

There is no doubt, however, that today the name is universally associated with W. J. Roué's schooner, *Bluenose*, now both a Nova Scotian and Canadian icon.

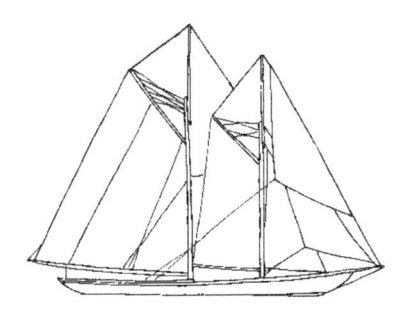

Appendix

Highlights: W. J. (Bill) Roué

1879	April 27	Born in Halifax, Nova Scotia.
1896		Leaves school and works for wholesale grocery firm, earning $100 annually. Takes classes in mechanical drafting at Victoria School of Art and Design.
		Receives an old Dixon-Kemp (*Yachting Architecture*), the naval architect's bible, from Frank H. Bell.
1897	June 27	Becomes member of the Royal Nova Scotia Yacht Squadron for a $10 fee.
1903		Joins family firm, Roué Carbonated Waters, Ltd., as a junior clerk.
1907		Designs his first mathematically calculated yacht for Frank H. Bell.
1908		Marries Winnifred Conrod and moves across the harbour to 23 James Street, Dartmouth, Nova Scotia.

1909	Spring	Frank H. Bell's yacht, *Babette*, is launched in Halifax.
1910	May 23	Birth of James Frederick.
1913	July 14	Birth of twins, Harry, and William F., who dies at birth.
1916	Sept. 9	Birth of Frances Grace.
1920	Fall	Receives contract from Bluenose Schooner Company of Lunenburg to design contender for the International Fishermen's Trophy.
1921	Mar. 26	*Bluenose* launched in Lunenburg, Nova Scotia.
	Oct.	*Bluenose* wins International Fishermen's Trophy
	Dec. 30	Receives a plaque and gift of recognition from the citizens of Dartmouth.
1922		Designs the Star Class, later renamed Roué 20.
1924		James Roué (father) dies.
		Becomes president of Roué's Carbonated Waters, Ltd.
1929		Sells Roué's Carbonated Waters, Ltd. to Bluenose Beverage Company. Remains part-time with Bluenose Beverage as a consultant, and establishes naval architect office on Barrington Street, Halifax.
1934		Leaves Bluenose Beverage Company to become a full-time naval architect.
		Moves to City Island, New York, to work

		in the firm of Ford, Payne, and W. J. Roué.
1936	Oct.	Moves back to Dartmouth.
1944		Moves office to Hollis Street in Halifax.
		Designs Bluenose Class.
1948		Moves office to James Street home, Dartmouth.
1949	Aug.	*Halifax Herald* announces the International Bluenose Class Championship annual competition.
1954		Winnifred Conrod Roué (Mrs. W. J.) dies.
		Honoured by the Armdale Yacht Club.
1963	Feb. 27	Helps drive golden spike into keel of *Bluenose II* at Smith and Rhuland Shipyards, Lunenburg.
	June 18	Honoured by the Royal Nova Scotia Yacht Squadron.
	July 23	*Bluenose II* launched in Lunenburg.
1970	Jan. 14	Dies at the age of 90 in his home, 23 James Street, Dartmouth.

W. J. Roué Designs

Following is a partial list of designs by W. J. Roué. The names of all the vessels are not known since they were usually named just prior to launching. As this list was compiled from very old documents after Mr. Roué's death, there are some blanks. For further information, please contact the author.

#	TYPE	DESIGNED FOR	NAME	LOA/LWL	YEAR
003	Yawl	F.H. Bell	*Babette*		
004	Yawl	Dr. Anderson		/27'	
006	Sloop	E.F. Zwicker	*Rowdy*	/19'	
015		National Fish Co.		/55'	1918
017	Fishing Schooner	Angus Walters	*Bluenose*	143'/110'	1921
020	Yacht	RNSYS		28'/20'	
022	Sloop	Chas. Bell		21'9"/17'	
023		J.A. Weingart			
024	R Class Sloop	A.A. Haliburton		35'/	
026	Schooner			/104'	
027	Sailing Dinghy			14'/	
029	One Class	RCYC			
030	Skiff Class	RNSYS			
032	Working Boat	Maritime Tel & Tel			

#	TYPE	DESIGNED FOR	NAME	LOA/LWL	YEAR
035	Schooner	Ford & Payne	Northern Light	/34'	
039	Ferry	N.S.H. Board		67'/60'	
040	Cruising Schooner	Wm.H.Judson.		49'6"/39'	1940
043	Auto Ferry	Caribou-Wood Isl.		160'/	
045A	Sloop	E.Bell/Dr.F.Lessel			
045B	Cruising Schooner	E.A. Bell			
048	Fishing Vessel			/112'	1924
051	Cruising Schooner	P.F. Burr		56'/45'6"	
052	Cruising Schooner	J.H. Winfield		100'/78'	
053A	Yawl	J.S. Taylor	Zetes		1952
053B		Jas.W. Barnes			1920's
053C	Staysail Schooner	A.S. Bull			
053D	Schooner	J.B. Edgar	Haligonian		
053E	Cruising Schooner			41'/31'2"	
054	Pilot Schooner	Halifax Pilot Com		104'/81'	

#	TYPE	DESIGNED FOR	NAME	LOA/LWL	YEAR
055	Fishing Schooner	E.W. Day & Co.		99'10"/78'1"	
058	Schooner	Shelburne Ship Bldr		99'9"/78'6"	
060A	Auto Ferry	NS Dept of Hwys	*Pont Canseau*		
060B		Cooke Bros.			
061	R Class Sloop			39'7.5"/26'	
062	Sloop	G.H. Godderham	*Acadia*		
065	Aux. Launch	Ernest Brooks		40'/	
066A	Sloop	G.S. Stairs			
066B	Ketch	Walter Molson			
067	Yawl	Horace Mann	*Flying Spray*	37'/28'	1926
068	Auto Ferry	NSHB			
069	Auto Ferry	NS Dept of Hwys	*Breton*		1949
071	Pilot Vessel	Halifax Pilot Com		106'6"/85'	
073	Schooner			151'/118'	
076	Schooner			65'/50'	

#	TYPE	DESIGNED FOR	NAME	LOA/LWL	YEAR
077	Auto Ferry	NS Dept of Hwys	*Charles Tupper*	100'/90'	
077A	Power Launch	Canada Customs		/60'	
078	Yacht	J.H.Winfield		65'/	
079	One Design	RNSYS		/30'	1936
081	Yawl	C.O.Stillman		42'/	
084	Racing Sloop	G.H.Gooderham	*Valeria*	48'3"/30'	
085	Cruising Launch	Etherington Bldg.		/40'	
087	Bluenose Class	John Molson		23'2.5"/	1957
089	Schooner	Walter Molson	*Caprice*	75'/57'6"	
091	Auto Ferry	Cape Sable, NS	*E. M. Rhode*	62'6"/60'	1949
092	Duty Boat	St. John Harbour		50'/	
096	Ferry	St. John Steamship		126'/120'	
098	Ketch	P.E. Nobbs		49'9"/40'	
099	Schooner	J.H. Winfield		65'/50'	
100	Ketch	Prof. MacKenzie		37'4"/30'	
101	Ketch	Dr.F. Barthleman		35'/29'2"	

#	TYPE	DESIGNED FOR	NAME	LOA/LWL	YEAR
104	Ketch	D.M. Hodgson		69'/52'6"	
105	Ferry	St. John	Loyalist	125'/115'	
106	Ketch	C.P. Cox		37'/30'	
107	Ketch	J.H. Winfield		52'6"/	
108	Cat Boat		Felix	23'4.5"/22'3'	
109	Launch	Fishery Patrol		50'/	
111	Racing Sloop			69'3"/45'	1934
112	Ketch	L.M. Wiloon		41'7.5"/35'	
116	12' Motor Launch	Fishery Patrol	Venning		
123	Yawl	Pearson McCurdy		/33"	1950
124	Sloop	MacKeen/Dobson	Eskasoni		1937
125	Schooner	Dept of Defence		/111'	
126	Freight Vessel			145'/	
126A	Sloop	Victor Mader	Audrey		1921
127	Motor Launch	Major R.E.Balders		31'6"/30'	
127A	Ketch	C.P. Cox		/30'	
128	Ketch	C.P. Cox		37'/30'	

#	TYPE	DESIGNED FOR	NAME	LOA/LWL	YEAR
129	Cruiser			/58'	
130	Yawl			62'10"/45'	
131	Twin Screw Launch	C.J. Osman			1938
131A		Dept. of Hwys		47'4"/45'	
132	Freight Vessel	J.A. Weingart		129'3"/121'4"	
137	Auto Ferry	Barrington	*Joseph Howe*	87'/78'	
139	Speed Launch	Fisheries Patrol		24'/	
140	Speed Launch	Fisheries Patrol		24'/	
141	Launch	Fisherman Loan Brd		45'/	
142	Launch	Fisherman Loan Brd		38'/	
143	Double End Ferry	Northumberland		160'/150'	1939
144	Launch	H.G. Stairs		/38'	
146	Ferry	Strait of Canso	*John Cabot*	130'/120'	1946
147	Pilot Boat	North Sydney			1942
148	Pilot Boat	Halifax Harbour			

#	TYPE	DESIGNED FOR	NAME	LOA/LWL	YEAR
149	Ferry	Hfx. to Dartmouth		149'/135'	
151	Pilot Boat	Hfx. Pilot Service		54'1.5"/52'	1952
153	Freight Schooner			185'/	
154	Freight Vessel	Natural Resources		135'1.5"/130'	
156	Sectional Barge	UK War Transport		/72'	1943
157	Wooden Tug	UK War Transport		/65'	
158	Fishing Vessel	Dept. of Fisheries	J.J. Cowie	67'1"/60'	1950
161	Bluenose Class			23'2.5"/16'	1948
162	Dragger			63'5"/60'	1948
163	Wooden Tug	UK War Transport		/65'	
164	One Design	N.Y.Y.C.		/30'	1945
165	Schooner	U.N.R.R.A.		65'/	1945
166	Launch	Canada Customs			
167	Auto Ferry	NS Dept of Hwys		47'/41'2"	

#	TYPE	DESIGNED FOR	NAME	LOA/LWL	YEAR
168	One Design	R.N.S.Y.S.	*Marita*	33'/23'	1940
169	Pilot Boat	NS Dept of Hwys			1953
170	Pilot Boat	Englishtown	*Highland Lass*		1951
170A	Roue 20 Redesign				1949
171	Sloop	Kinley		34'9"/24'	
172	Twin Screw Launch	Don Raymond		55'2"/52'6"	1955
172A	One Design			/20'	1950
173	Sloop	Bill Barnes		31'9"/22'	1948
174	Racing Sloop	R.N.S.Y.S.		39'9"/25'	1948
175	Freighter	John Etherington		149'10"/145'	1948
176	Ketch	J.H. Winfield		38'9"/28'	1949
177	Cruiser			/40'	1948
177A	Lifeboat	Lunenburg Foundry		/16'	
177B	Patrol Boat			38'6"/35'	1948
178	Roue 20				1950
179	Ketch			38'/30'	1948

#	TYPE	DESIGNED FOR	NAME	LOA/LWL	YEAR
180	Auto Ferry	Govt. of Nfld.		/51'4"	1951
180A	Ketch	R.P. Bell			
180B	Tancook Whaler			36'6"/29'6"	1950
181	Patrol Boat	Dept. Internal Rev.		42'1"/	
183	Yawl	W.W. Slocum	*Flying Spray II*	/31'	1952
186	Ferry	Placentia Harbour		64'8"/56'8"	1952
187	Bluenose Jr.			36'6"/27'6"	1953
188	Schooner	Dr. A.L. Murphy	*Mary J.*		1953
189	Auto Ferry	NS Dept. of Works		78'/70'	1953
190	Barge			50'/	1953
191	Scow	Grand Passage		45'/	1953
192	Ferry	Westport-Freeport		55'/	1953
196	Towing Scow	Lahave Ferry		51'	1955
198	Tug Boat	Smith & Rhuland		/40'	1954
198A	Sloop	Harry Thompson		38'/28'	1955
199	Sloop	Capt. C.A. Copelin		32'9"/25'	1955

#	TYPE	DESIGNED FOR	NAME	LOA/LWL	YEAR
200	Sloop	Harry Thompson		45'9"/34'	1955
201	Centreboard Ketch	Morley Taylor		42'6"/32'	1955
203		Ind.Shipping Co		123'/	1959
205	Work Boat	Dept. of Works		/60'	1956
206	Sloop	Harry Thompson		/34'	
208	Cape Island			26'7"/	1958
209	Sloop	Harry Thompson		44'6"/34'6"	1956
210	Auto Ferry	Tancook-Chester		70'/65'	1959
267	Schooner	Smith & Rhuland	*Bluenose II*	143'/	1959
717	Cruising Cutter			45'4.5"/	1935
723	Ketch			32'/	1934
724	Schooner			/55'	1935
725	Cruising Launch			/30'	
726	One Design	R.N.S.Y.S.		/15'	
727	Twin Screw Launch			/58'	1935

#	TYPE	DESIGNED FOR	NAME	LOA/LWL	YEAR
731	One Design			24'3.5"/16'	
735	Cruising Cutter			50'6"/35'	
741	Yawl		*Duchess*		
743	Ketch				
777	8 Metre Yacht				1929
900	3 Mast Schooner	Canadian Navy	*Venture*	140'/	1920's
901		Michael Dwyer	*Atlanta*		1945
902	Cape Island	R.P. Bell			
904	Motor Boat	Senator Pratt			
905		E.A. Bell			
906	Ferry Boat	Hfx to Dartmouth			
907	R Class		*Vengeance*		
909	Ketch	J.W. Knox			1953
910	Sloop	S. & J. Wurts	*Hayseed IV*		1956
911	Auto Ferry	Tiverton			
912	Coastal Schooner			60'/50'	

Highlights: *Bluenose*

1920	Fall	Bluenose Schooner Co. commissions W. J. Roué to design a winning vessel for the second International Fishermen's races. Roué designs *Bluenose,* Roué Plan #17.
1921	Mar. 26	Launched in Lunenburg, Nova Scotia.
	Apr. 15	Sets sail for the Grand Banks.
	Oct.	Defeats American challenger, *Elsie*, in Halifax, Nova Scotia. Wins International Fishermen's Trophy.
1922	Oct.	Defeats American challenger, *Henry Ford*, in Gloucester, Massachusetts. Wins International Fishermen's Trophy.
1923	Oct.	Competes with American challenger, *Columbia*, in Halifax. Ruled no contest. International Fishermen's Trophy is not awarded.
1929	Jan. 6	Government of Canada issues 50¢ commemorative *Bluenose* postage stamp.
1930	Oct.	Loses Lipton Cup series to American contender, *Gertrude L. Thebaud*, in Gloucester.
1931	Oct.	Defeats *Gertrude L. Thebaud* in Halifax. Wins the International Fishermen's Trophy.
1933		Represents Canada at Chicago World's Fair, Chicago, Illinois.
1934		Spends several months in Toronto, Ontario.

1935		Sails to England for King George V and Queen Mary's Silver Jubilee.
1936		Diesel engines are installed, sails are removed.
1937	Jan. 1	Government of Canada mints the first *Bluenose* dime.
1938	Oct.	Defeats American challenger, *Gertrude L. Thebaud*, in Gloucester. Wins International Fishermen's Trophy.
1942		Sold to the West Indies Trading Co., and carries cargo in the West Indies.
1946	Jan. 29	Sinks off Haiti.

Bluenose Racing Log

Following is a record of *Bluenose*'s official races.

1921   International Fishermen's Trophy-Halifax, Nova Scotia

    #1-Oct. 22   *Bluenose*   1:32:10
                      Elsie   1:45:25

    #2-Oct. 24   *Bluenose*   12:09:16
                      Elsie   12:18:47

Bluenose was the series winner.

1922   International Fishermen's Trophy-Gloucester, Massachusetts

    #1-Oct. 23   *Henry Ford*   4:01:31
                      Bluenose   4:04:00

    #2-Oct. 24   *Bluenose*   4:57:41
                      Henry Ford   5:05:04

    #3-Oct. 25   *Bluenose*   4:48:38
                      Henry Ford   5:05:04

Bluenose was the series winner.

1923   International Fishermen's Trophy-Halifax, Nova Scotia

    #1-Oct. 29   *Bluenose*   1:43:42
                      Columbia   1:45:02

    #2-Nov. 01   *Bluenose*   5:36:02
                      Columbia   5:38:48

Ruled "No Contest" after a dispute over the rules.

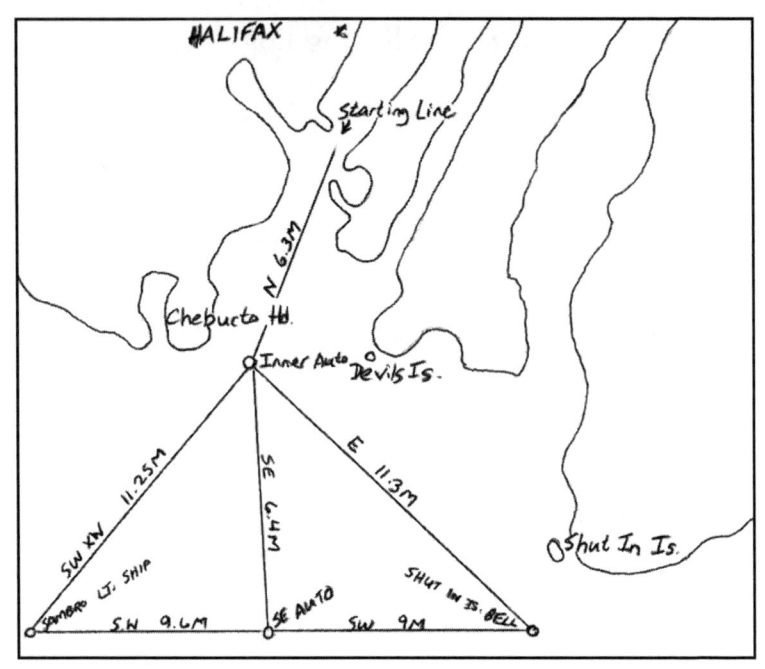

1921 International Fishermen's Trophy race course, Halifax, N.S.

1930   Sir Thomas Lipton Cup-Gloucester, Massachusetts

     #1-Oct. 09   *Gertrude L. Thebaud*   3:19:40
                    Bluenose   3:55:17

     #2-Oct. 18   *Gertrude L. Thebaud*   2:17:09
                    Bluenose   2:25:03

     Gertrude L. Thebaud was the series winner.

1931   International Fishermen's Trophy-Halifax, Nova Scotia

     #1-Oct. 19   *Bluenose*   2:53:49
                    Gertrude L. Thebaud   3:26:15

     #2-Oct.20   *Bluenose*   2:33:12
                   Gertrude L. Thebaud   2:48:13

     Bluenose was the series winner.

1938   International Fishermen's Trophy-Gloucester, Massachusetts

     #1-Oct. 09   *Gertrude L. Thebaud*   0:2:56

     #2-Oct. 13   *Bluenose*   0:12:00

     #3-Oct. 23   *Bluenose*   0:6:39

     #4-Oct. 24   *Gertrude L. Thebaud*   0:5:00

     #5-Oct. 26   *Bluenose*   0:2:50

Bluenose was the series winner. (Times given in this instance show the margin of victory).

Highlights: *Bluenose II*

1962		Commissioned by Oland & Son, Limited, Halifax, Nova Scotia.
1963	July 23	Launched in Lunenburg, Nova Scotia.
1967		Serves as Canada's official host ship at Expo '67, Montréal, Québec.
1971	Sept. 7	Sold to the Province of Nova Scotia for one dollar.
1972		Town of Lunenburg, launches Save the *Bluenose II* campaign to finance a $250,000 refit.
1974		Makes her first voyage as Nova Scotia's Ambassador. Sails to Norfolk, Virginia, then works her way up the eastern seaboard.
1975	Spring	Makes a six week promotional tour of Canada's interior and the United States, through the St. Lawrence River and Great Lakes.
	Summer	Receives new berth at Historic Properties, Halifax.
1976		Participates in extensive tour of American seaports, and Operation Sail, New York City, as part of the U.S. bicentennial celebrations.
1978	Spring	Sails first to Bermuda, then up the U.S. eastern seaboard visiting twelve ports.
1984		Serves as Canada's official host ship for the gathering of International Sail training

		ships at Halifax and Sydney, Nova Scotia, and Québec City, Québec.
1985-86		Visits Expo '86, Vancouver, British Columbia, on an 18-month voyage.
1988	Apr.	Province of Nova Scotia issues the first *Bluenose* license plate.
	Nov.	Canada Post issues a commemorative stamp honouring Captain Angus Walters.
1992		Receives a plaque from Canada Post during Canada's 125th anniversary celebrations.
		St. Lawrence Seaway tour includes stops in Toronto, Montréal, and Québec City.
1994	Mar. 17	Province of Nova Scotia announces it will no longer sail *Bluenose II*.
	Aug. 26	Federal government wants a sailing *Bluenose II* available for G-7 summit to be held in Halifax, June, 1995.
	Sept. 28	Bluenose II Preservation Trust established to oversee refit with federal and provincial funding, and private contributions.
1995	Jan. 4	Restoration work begins by Snyder's Shipyard Ltd., in Lunenburg.
	Apr.	Bluenose II Preservation Trust chooses Wayne Walters as captain.
	May 8	Relaunched in Lunenburg.
	May 28	Recommissioned in Lunenburg.
	June	Participates in G-7 summit, Halifax.

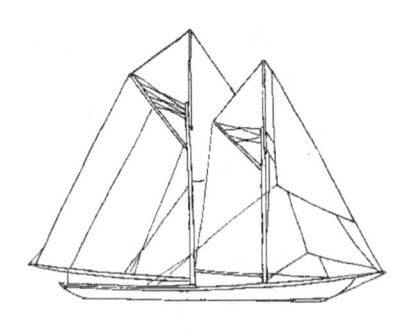

References

Bluenose Pride Seafaring Cooperative. *Bluenose Pride* brochure. 1995.

Dartmouth (N.S.) Free Press, 23 June 1960.

Dartmouth (N.S.) Free Press, 4 August 1966.

Dartmouth (N.S.) Free Press, 27 July 1967.

Emery, H.G. and Brewster, K.G. *New Century Dictionary of the English Language.* New York: D. Appleton-Century, 1942.

Halifax Herald:

> 21 March 1921; 25 March 1921; 26 March 1921; 28 March 1921;
>
> 30 March 1921;13 October 1921; 14 October 1921; 18 October 1921;
>
> 19 October 1921; 24 October 1921; 25 October 1921; 24 October 1938
>
> 27 October 1938; 31 January 1946;14 June 1963; 30 September 1967; 16 May 1972.

Hamilton, Ross. *Prominent Men of Canada*. National Publishing Co., 1931.

Isaacs, I.J. *Halifax: The Capital of Nova Scotia.* 1909.

Merkel, Andrew. *Schooner Bluenose.* Toronto: The Ryerson Press, 1948.

Payzant, Joan and Lewis. *Like a Weavers Shuttle.* Halifax: NIMBUS Publishing, 1979.

Province of Nova Scotia, Dept. of Tourism & Culture. *Bluenose II* pamphlet.

Roué, W. J., personal files.

Spray Magazine, Volume 10, No. 1.

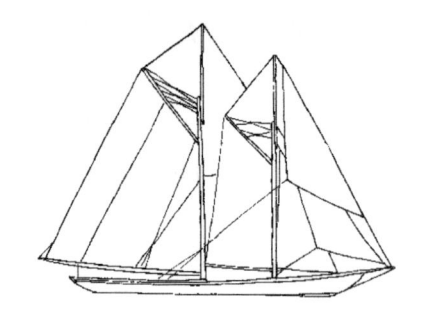

Acknowledgements

Dorothy Mae (Poirier) Roué
Lawrence James Roué
Jeanne Francis (Roué) Robinson
The late James Frederick Roué
The late William James Roué
Public Archives of Nova Scotia
The Halifax City Library, Research Dept.
The Halifax Herald Ltd.
Wilfred Moore
Philip Snyder
Al Chaddock
Ed Murphy
Al Stevens, City of Halifax
The Hon. Robbie Harrison, Province of Nova Scotia

NEW SINCE 1995
May 1995 to May 2002

Bluenose II leading the Tall Ships Parade in Halifax, July 24, 2000. (Photo by Joan Roué.)

Nearly seven years have passed since the first edition of this book was released. It has been a busy time indeed, with posthumous honours and accolades bestowed on William James Roué and his accomplishments; on the *Bluenose*; and on the continued accomplishments of *Bluenose II*. This truly is a book with a happy ending.

For the Roué family, it has been most gratifying to see the revival of appreciation for the talents of W.J. Roué. His Design No. 17, or *Bluenose* as we know it, is a constant reminder of his legacy. Every time we see the back of a Canadian 10-cent piece or a Nova Scotia vehicle license plate or indeed *Bluenose II* sailing proudly, we feel a deep sense of heritage that is impossible to describe in words.

But it was a beautiful sunny afternoon in Halifax, Nova Scotia in July 1998 that truly left us speechless. This was the occasion of the unveiling of a commemorative stamp bearing the image of William J. Roué—a stamp issued by Canada Post to commemorate his life and accomplishments. The stamp was in circulation for one year and you can rest assured that each and every piece of mail I sent that year proudly displayed the W.J. Roué stamp—again instilling a sense of familial pride.

The official news release from Canada Post was entitled "Canada Post honours designer/creator of the legendary schooner, the *Bluenose*." Excerpts follow:

> OTTAWA – Canada Post will be honouring the greatest designer of wooden sailing vessels in Canadian history, and one of the most talented in the world...on July 24, the Corporation will issue a single stamp to commemorate the life and achievements of William Roué, designer of the legendary schooner *Bluenose*.
>
> The stamp design superimposes a head-and-shoulders image of Roué over a recreation of the "1929 *Bluenose* stamp". The denomination of the *Bluenose* stamp has been changed from the original 50¢ to 45¢. Roué's image is produced by lithography while the original 1929 elements were created by steel-engraving. The designer, Louis. C. Hébert of Montreal, says "we can see that Roué is looking into the distance—away from the *Bluenose*—like a visionary."

Like its predecessor, the *Bluenose* part of the stamp was created in shades of blue on a white background while the Roué image was imposed on the left side of the stamp and presented in four-colour pastel. "A unique two-stage process" was the technical description given me at the time. "Beautiful" is perhaps the best way to describe it in layman's terms.

Another note of interest is that the head-and-shoulders image used on the stamp was taken from a family photo where my great-grandfather was pictured with his wife, my great-grandmother Winifred. So it is particularly heart-warming on a personal note to know that the "visionary" look described by the stamp designer was actually captured when my great-grandfather was sharing a moment with his wife.

Several hundred people were on hand for the stamp's unveiling, including four generations of my family, members of the crew of the original *Bluenose*, and several dignitaries including The Honourable Alfonso Gagliano, minister responsible for Canada Post and The Honourable Wilfred P. Moore, Q.C., Senator of Canada.

For me, it was one of those "larger than life" days. Yet another of those days is surely in the near future as we anticipate the opening of the William J. Roué Reading Room in Lunenburg, Nova Scotia. This will be a place where all Roué and nautical enthusiasts can go to study or research the seafaring tradition and shipbuilding industry in Nova Scotia. Full scale Roué drawings will be on display for all to enjoy as well as a detailed electronic database of his works.

Although he was a humble man, I can assure you W.J. Roué's greatest glory today would rest in the endurance of his designs, particularly the Bluenose Class which has been sailing for over 50 years and is currently seeing a revival in new construction, and the Roué 20 design, now over 80 years old, many of which still grace the waterways of the Maritime provinces and beyond.

And he would be proud of the continued successes of *Bluenose II*, a Canadian icon that was doomed only seven short years ago. We can all thank our lucky stars for the efforts of those involved with the *Bluenose II* Preservation Trust, particularly the passionate leadership of volunteer chairman Wilfred P. Moore. I urge you to visit their stores in either Lunenburg, Nova Scotia or on the downtown waterfront in Halifax, Nova Scotia, or to visit them on the world wide web at http://www.bluenose2.ns.ca. The support they receive through these venues is what keeps our favourite schooner sailing.

When you look at what she has accomplished in the last seven years there can be absolutely no doubt that we need to keep her sailing.

Bluenose II has hosted the most powerful leaders of the world, visiting ports worldwide as an ambassador for Nova Scotia and for Canada. Most recently, on March 15, 2002, the Royal Canadian Mint officially acknowledged what all Canadians had assumed for 65 years—that the "two masted schooner" that has graced the back of the Canadian 10-cent piece since 1937, is indeed *Bluenose*. Yet another tribute to the efforts of the *Bluenose II* Preservation Trust.

For me, this project is ongoing and thanks to the passion of those who own, have owned, or simply admire Roué vessels, this is a story that continues to unfold. I am constantly amazed by the sheer breadth of recognition W.J. Roué still commands. Countless phone calls, letters and e-mails have been received from people worldwide who have recognized a description offered from this book, a newspaper story, television or radio story.

We know there is a "Bird Boat" (Design No. 79) under restoration in British Columbia. We have discovered members of the Tampa Yacht & Country Club in Florida still revere the life and talents of W.J. Roué, designer of *Little Haligonian*, the most famous vessel ever to sail from their club and winner of countless races to Havana. We know there is another Roué-designed schooner under restoration in St. Augustine, Florida. And more...

To that end, and with the global power of the internet, we implore anyone who has knowledge pertaining to past or present Roué designs to share those facts or stories with us through our official W.J. Roué web site at http://www.wjroue.com.

And so, it seems, this little book called *A Spirit Deep Within*, named at the time to describe the inexplicable spirit W.J. Roué drew from in his genius, has stirred a spirit deep within many.

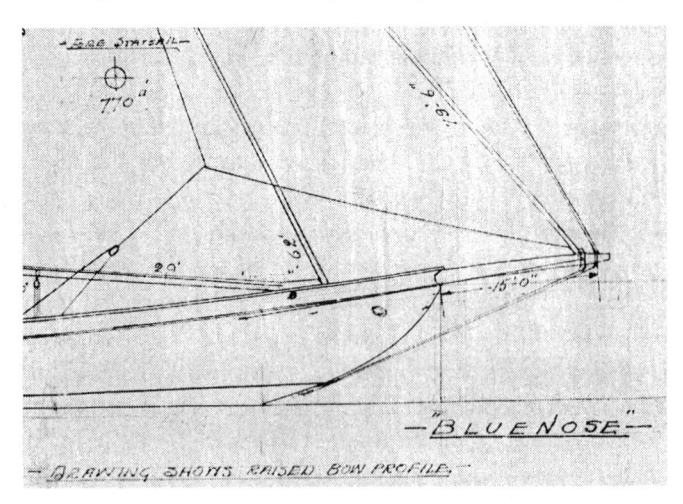

The original drawing of the controversial bow alteration on *Bluenose*. Many felt this change was the reason for her great speed, while Roué himself felt it would, if anything, slow her down.

(Courtesy Bluenose II Preservation Trust ©)

BLUENOSE and *BLUENOSE II* Highlights
Addendum to pages 95-96

1995	Host Vessel for the Economic Summit meeting of the Leaders of the G-7 countries at Halifax, Nova Scotia.
1996	Visited Gloucester, Mass., and hosted a reunion of crewmembers of the original *Bluenose* and of *Gertrude L. Thebaud*.
1997	First ship to pass under the Confederation Bridge (linking Prince Edward Island to the mainland of Canada) upon its opening on May 31.
1997	Conducted a National Tour, including a visit to Thunder Bay, Ontario, her deepest sail into Canada's heartland.
1998	Visited the waters off Haiti where *Bluenose* foundered on January 28, 1946, and cast a wreath of remembrance.
1999	Participated in Newfoundland's "Soiree '99" in celebration of that province's 50th Anniversary of Confederation, including visits to St. John's, Harbour Breton and Marystown.
2000 July 20	Royal Canadian Mint issued $20 collector's hologram coin featuring *Bluenose*
2000 July	Participated in "Tall Ships 2000," a gathering of the world's fleet, including visits to Bermuda, ports along the Eastern Seaboard of USA, New Brunswick and Quebec, and led the Parade of Sail in Halifax Harbour in Canada's largest nautical celebration of the new millennium.
2001 Mar 26	80th Anniversary of *Bluenose* acknowledged in Canadian Senate.
2001 Apr 2	World premiere of *Requiem for a Queen*, a 60-minute made for television *Bluenose* documentary, on History Television cable network.

2001	Participated in American Sail Training Association's "Great Lakes Tall Ships Challenge," including visits to Kingston, Port Colborne, Cleveland, Sarnia, Windsor, Detroit and Bay City.
2001	Hosted pilots and spouses of 434 *Bluenose* Squadron (Combat Support) of Greenwood, Nova Scotia, for a sail off Lunenburg which included a fly pass by jets of this historic squadron, whose aircraft bear an image of the ship on their tail fins.
2002 Mar 15	*Bluenose* is officially acknowledged by the Royal Canadian Mint as the vessel that has been on the back of the Canadian 10-cent piece since 1937.

William J. Roué Highlights
Addendum to pages 81-83

1997	*A Toast to William Roué* gala event at the Royal Nova Scotia Yacht Squadron in Halifax, Nova Scotia, on the occasion of the 75th anniversary of the Roué 20 (Design # 20).
1998	William J. Roué stamp issued by Canada Post
2002	Official opening of the William J. Roué Reading Room in Lunenburg, Nova Scotia, offering a unique collection of nautical books and a comprehensive body of work of William J. Roué, including drawings.
2002	Launching of the Official William J. Roué web site at http://www.wjroue.com.